THE 21 LAWS
OF SURVIVING A
GENTLEMEN'S
CLUB

THE 21 LAWS OF SURVIVING A GENTLEMEN'S CLUB

Darius Allen

Varsity Club

PUBLISHED BY VARSITY CLUB PUBLISHING
a division of Varsity Club Enterprises, LLC.

www.varsityclubinc.com

Varsity Club

is a registered trademark of Varsity Club Enterprises, LLC.
Manufactured and printed in the United States of America
Library of Congress Cataloging in Publication Data

The 21 Laws of Surviving a Gentlemen's Club/Darius Allen
1. Sex 2. Self-Help & Psychology
3. Social Philosophy 4. Economics

Library of Congress Control Number: 2016910743

ISBN: 978-0-9974320-0-8

Cover design and Illustrations by Jesse Gonzales
Edited by Trojans

THIS BOOK IS DEDICATED TO YOU BRAVE SOULS WHO
ENTER A GENTLEMEN'S CLUB AND REALIZE THE
SPOTLIGHT IS NOT ON THE STAGE—IT'S ON YOU.

CONTENTS

Survivor's Note

In this book, the names "gentlemen's club" and "strip club" are used interchangeably. You can waste your time on the particulars, but a jungle is a jungle. Some gentlemen club owners and managers may disagree with this decision. It makes sense. The last thing they want is the association with establishments that are considered raunchy or so-called urban. But the focus is not on their branding and marketing techniques. The focus is on stripping away the facade and glamorization of the strip club industry.

As far as the title of this book, the emphasis is on the word *gentlemen*. The very word evokes a certain type of attitude and behavior. It's those qualities that will allow you to understand the laws, and adapt to any challenge in the jungle, regardless of the type of club and location.

By the way, if you're wondering who I am and how I could write this book; I'm a survivor. You may have seen me in the shadows, enjoying a cocktail.

Preface

Don't fool yourself; the primary goal is to obtain a lap dance that's worth the price. That's the holy grail; it's the alpha and omega of the gentlemen's club. It can vary from low mileage to high mileage, but in essence, it doesn't matter as long as getting the most "bang for your buck" is the basis of your agenda. Without a doubt, within the rules of engagement, the lap dance provides the best value for your visit. However, most of you have been led astray. You've been duped, brainwashed, and bamboozled into being a helpless spectator. You visit a club to shoot the breeze, enjoy a casual drink, and tip without purpose. Your primary goal is to earn the reputation of a rainmaker and sneak in a selfie with a stripper in the background as an extra.

It's time to sound the alarm and go over the basics. Every visitor to a gentlemen's club needs to understand the premise of this motivational theory. Based on the hedonistic desire to experience all five senses (sight, hearing, smell, touch, and taste), everything flows and revolves around the Patron's Hierarchy of Needs (see Fig. 1).

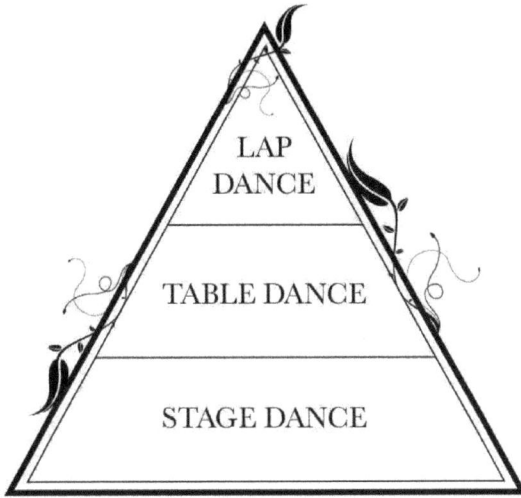

Fig. 1. Patron's Hierarchy of Needs

The three levels enable the patron to utilize those five senses to their maximum and at the very top of the pyramid is the coveted lap dance. In a traditional sense, the hierarchy is best explained through the following chronological steps:

SIGHT AND HEARING

1. The pyramid begins with the patron's basic physiological need to observe the female body in motion, wearing a sexy outfit, and dancing erotically to the sounds of music (Stage Dance).

SIGHT, HEARING, AND SMELL

2. Once a patron is visually stimulated and has identified a target, the natural instinct is to request a closer, more intimate look, allowing the patron to hear her soothing voice and smell her seductive scent (Table Dance).

SIGHT, HEARING, SMELL, TOUCH, AND THE FANTASY OF TASTE

3. Finally, the patron and the target escape to a dark corner and enjoy a lively encounter that satisfies all five senses. The patron is close enough to see her goose bumps, and hear every explicit whisper underneath the backdrop of a sensual song. At the same time, caressing her skin and fantasizing about tasting her forbidden fruit (Lap Dance).

Now, that wasn't too hard, was it? This theory would seem like common sense. But given the intoxicating influence of hip hop and its strip club anthems, most are caught up in the hoopla of making it rain and having an "all eyes on me" mentality inside the club. The lap dance has become a distraction from self-promotion and vanity, instead of a lustful pursuit. It's hard to believe, but out of all places, the gentlemen's club has been infiltrated by rampant narcissism. Sadly, it's to the point where men are craving to be the center of attention in a room full of strippers. Some even try to find an excuse to get on stage and steal the spotlight. But the more seasoned clientele conceal their predacious gaze in the shadows and admire the pole work over a signature cocktail. He's aware of the value of getting a lap dance that heightens all five senses and understands that a gentlemen's club is a sacred layer of sexuality where the stripper is the main attraction, and focusing on the hierarchy of needs is necessary to enhance the experience.

The 21 Laws of Surviving a Gentlemen's Club was written to redirect the attention back towards the physical interaction between a patron and a stripper, and also examine the inner working of a social environment that wants to swallow up your money and spit you out. You must realize that the behavior of the average strip club patron is evolving before your eyes—and this spells danger. Many see nothing wrong with going against the universal strip club law of reciprocity:

You give her scratch, and she'll scratch your back.

This law is on the verge of being abolished —by a new silent majority. But like the Great Pyramid of Giza, the hierarchy of needs was built to stand the test of time. This pyramid will weather the storm of a culture of misguided patrons who treat a gentlemen's club like a trendy nightclub, lounge, or popular restaurant chain. There is a clear difference! Unfortunately, many need to be reminded of the obvious (see Fig. 1).

The words, examples, and metaphors contained in this book are a literary representation of what you're up against in the jungle; the appropriate name that represents the predatory nature of the environment. Given that a gentlemen's club is advertised as a fantasyland, the more realistically and logically we analyze the intricacies, the better.

This book will serve as a wake-up call; a fiery pep talk before a planned trip, a conversation starter for the bold, and a syllabus for all rookies:

Laws 1-8: The Fundamentals
Laws 9-15: Survival Strategies
Laws 16-21: Discourses

Add the laws together and you have a strip club handbook that focuses on priority and purpose.

Seriously, why are you there?

You're not visiting a club for the drink specials. You're not there to watch the ballgame. Certainly, don't say that you're there to sample the various hookah flavors. If you're there to visit a special guest DJ, do yourself a favor and keep that a secret. Lastly, please don't say that you're there for Taco Tuesday or the buffalo wings.

There is only one thing that should be

looked up and down, and it's not the food menu. The main dish should always be a sexy stripper served with a side of lap dance. Period!

If you choose to deviate from the laws, that's your prerogative, but keep in mind that you are involuntarily eroding the top of the pyramid.

That's why the increase of strippers that deem themselves "stage dancers" is no surprise. They conveniently remain on the stage, fill their bags with money, and avoid touches at all costs. Giving a lap dance is beneath them—talk about a stripper *Jedi mind trick*! This attitude is a direct result of patrons not sticking to the primary goal; once again it's obtaining a lap dance that's worth the price.

Consequently, waitresses and bartenders have taken notice of this lack of focus and are aiming to take advantage of it. Now, they're in the clubs emulating strippers and twerking for dollars. Why not? For them, it's easy money, and they don't mind blurring the lines as long as patrons are afraid to speak out—until now. This is the Age of the Stripper, and the hierarchy of needs highlights the three essential services that *only* they provide. If there was a constellation called Stripper, the pyramid would perfectly align with its brightest star: Lap Dance.

Those brave enough to work the pole should only occupy the stripper's territory. Waitresses and bartenders should stick to their job description and respect those at the top of the strip club food chain (see Fig. 2).

CASH → PATRON → BARTENDER → WAITRESS → STRIPPER

Fig. 2. Basic Strip Club Food Chain

Instead, some waitresses and bartenders would rather leech off of strippers like parasites, and compete for attention that should be directed to the stage. And on top of that, they have the nerve to look down on strippers; the ones who keep the entire industry alive. #RespectTheStripper.

Even if a club encourages this behavior, the question is who supports it? You. It's one thing to enjoy a party atmosphere, but never lose touch with the fact that you can't get any type of dance from a waitress or bartender. Do not allow their sneaky tactics and the additional services provided to divert your attention from the very reason the modern stripping industry exists; the sacred lap dance. Otherwise, you might as well go to a restaurant that serves terrible chicken wings and stare at waitresses that wear white tank tops and orange shorts. There's also a thing called the Internet which can provide more than enough *visual* entertainment.

The message is clear: if you continue to devalue the importance of the lap dance, don't be surprised if 15 years from now, the lap dance becomes nonexistent. Patrons will wander through the club wearing hazmat suits, examining strippers from afar, and treating what was once a sexual playground as a toxic environment of emasculation. A gentlemen's club will be a place where experiencing all five senses is the last thing on a patron's mind. The rub? You'll still be expected to tip generously.

Introduction

To live is to suffer, to survive is to find some
meaning in the suffering.

—Friedrich Nietzsche

The 21 laws are strictly about survival. Yes,
this is a matter of survival. Before you even think
about matching wits and gamesmanship with a
stripper, knowing that your survival is at stake is
paramount. You may believe that it's all fun and
games, but it's no fantasy when your money
disappears, and your *thirst* remains. Being on the
receiving end of an Air Dance is downright
depressing. Suffering through a VIP that you regret
paying for is devastating. Although the wounds on
your bank account may heal, the effect on your
psyche is permanent.

Outsiders and simpletons will scoff at the
use of the word survival, but for those who know, it's
as fitting as the strap on a stripper's stiletto.

To grasp the 21 laws successfully, one must
first take an honest look at the landscape. There are
several types of strip clubs: fully nude, topless,
bikini, or the newly created hybrids popping up
called exotic clubs (primarily, nightclubs with go-go

dancers). Some clubs only play hip hop's latest strip club anthems. And as far as rock music, you can always find a club in the middle of America playing the highly appropriate "Girls, Girls, Girls" by Mötley Crüe.

Each club offers its list of special features: full bar, cigars, champagne rooms, food menus, massage girls, porn stars, just to name a few. They also have their set of rules that may be broken depending on the stripper and the shift.

You have your mainstream chains like Déjà Vu, Cheetahs, and the Spearmint Rhino. There's Rick's Cabaret, a brand that trades on the Nasdaq —yes, you can buy shares instead of making it rain. There's the famous Sam's Hofbrau located in downtown Los Angeles, also known as the Cake Factory. In Hollywood, you can have a crazy time at a spot aptly called Crazy Girls. If you've turned on the radio, you may have heard about Miami's King of Diamonds, or Atlanta's Magic City, clubs referenced by rap artists such as Drake and Juicy J. There are even BYOB (bring your own booze) clubs all throughout Texas that are fully nude and don't close until 5:00 a.m.—imagine that.

It's impossible not to mention Las Vegas and its staple clubs like Sapphire and Crazy Horse III. Those clubs are mini coliseums with multiple VIP rooms; you can literally get lost in lust.

There is absolutely no shortage of strip clubs (it's a multibillion-dollar industry for a reason).

Variety is the spice of life, but when discussing the different types of clubs, the bottom line is often overshadowed by bells and whistles. Too often patrons fall victim to the glamorization and the allure of the strip club industry. Once you buy into the facade, proper perspective exits the back door.

Ask yourself this question: would you rather get bit by a Bushmaster snake or a Coral snake?

It doesn't matter.

A bite from either snake can be fatal, and that's the bottom line.

No matter the club, they're all jungles. Regardless of their names and status; never mind whatever is on their social media account, flyer or website; forget about the lyrics you hear in any rap song; they're all jungles full of wildlife and endless danger. The only major differences are the level of intensity and the population of ferocious predators within.

You have to watch out for carnivorous untamed felines—most covered in rosettes (tattoos); money tree (pole) dwelling primates; and the various species of the land roaming (Spearmint) rhino; BBW's (Big Beautiful Woman), PAWG's (Phat Ass White Girl), and juicy-thicks. There are Vultures that hover around the main floor waiting for you to slip up and expose your wounds. And you don't need to be close to the water to be attacked by a pack of Piranhas—just reserve a table and keep the bottles popping. You must also be on the lookout for poisonous snakes in fishnet dresses that slither around corners, tell beautiful lies, and strike when undetected—the jungle is full of surprises.

You can stroll into a dead club with only five strippers on stage and leave hours later, broke and despaired. A corn-fed stripper from Iowa can provide just as much venom as a tanned stripper from Florida. In addition, you can visit America's top 10 strip clubs and still walk away highly disappointed from the selection and the lack of customer service.

Don't get caught up in the hype. Always see a club for what it truly is; a jungle. Your challenge is to cut through the brush, survive the terrain, and avoid the infamous Walk of Shame.

The Walk of Shame? This phenomenon is rarely discussed, and that's for good reason.

Have you ever witnessed a pale-faced man escaping a club within an inch of his life? Embarrassedly, limping away, licking his wounds, and his pockets hemorrhaging from strippers gouging his funds. The once confident, charismatic smile he wore has now morphed into a lifeless, stoic stare as he hides his face like a celebrity fleeing the paparazzi. It's a morbid sight. That dreadful look of defeat can haunt a strip club amateur for months. His pride and bank account have been pillaged. In a few days, he will be hit with ATM withdrawal fees, adding insult to injury.

The Walk of Shame is real!

What about the rookie who is planning his first strip club excursion with the fellas while telling his parents a fib about going to a late night movie? Even though an inaugural trip to the strip club is a common rite of passage, fathers rarely get the invite to this ceremonious event. The young man's adrenaline is rushing while listening to the latest strip club anthem. He's worked hard for the $300 that rests in his pocket and is foolishly over-confident that he will only spend $100 for the time of his life; the rest is for flashing.

The rookie has a target, a stripper that he and his entourage have been following on various social media accounts. They drool over her twerk videos and bathroom selfies. In his mind, he has his plan of attack, but sadly, he will only be taking his cues from lyrics and rap videos. Finally, they enter, and he makes eye contact with his target—a stripper named Trouble, and her sinful curves are a problem.

Four hours later, he's begging a friend to borrow $40—his pockets are empty, his eyes are watery, and his heart is pounding. Despite his protest, they drag him out of the club and flee the vicinity. He survived his first trip, but it will take him months to recover from that Walk of Shame.

The brave souls who've entered a dimly lit, neon-tinted club quickly realize that the spotlight is not on the stage; it's on you. That's when you learn that you are the prey and survival is the name of the game.

   After all that, the only thing that matters is that you live to fight another day, or rather, you live to suffer another night. You've earned your stripes, and your jeans have been plastered with glitter like a badge of honor. You have officially found meaning in the suffering.

   You are a survivor.

THE 21 LAWS
OF SURVIVING A
GENTLEMEN'S
CLUB

LAW

1

KNOW THE WAYS
OF THE JUNGLE

This law is about situational awareness. To
know the ways of the jungle is to know the nature
of the jungle. A gentlemen's club is one of the most
voracious, capitalistic environments on Earth. Those
who enter this jungle clueless and slaphappy,
believing that they can escape unscathed, are sadly
mistaken. It's not a walk in the park. Being oblivious
to the traps in the jungle can lead you strolling into
a pit of quicksand. Ironically, death by quicksand is
usually due to thirst or starvation; not unlike that of
a 30-minute VIP tryst with a curvy stripper that
you're dying to take home.

Step through the doorway, you quickly
realize that this isn't exactly the Tarzan story from

your childhood. There is a definite role reversal in this storyline. In this adventure, Jane has tattoos, ass shots, and she's far from a damsel in distress. The jungle is her territory, and she's quite aware of her dominant position in it. Keeping a watchful eye for g-stringed predators like Jane is just one aspect of your awareness. Most importantly, you must be mindful of the prodding voices in your head that cloud your judgment and confuse your agenda. It takes shrewdness and clarity of thought to avoid the infamous Walk of Shame. Thousands of years of evolution have proven it difficult to think straight with asses twerking everywhere. Once your five senses are combined, words like discipline and restraint conveniently exit your train of thought. That's when your 15-minute VIP continues for another hour and your proposed budget, like the Titanic starts to sink into the red.

The unfortunate paradox of the gentlemen's club is that you spend money to have fun, but running out of money is no fun, and most of you reach your limit quicker than you'd like to. It's enough to drive you crazy and get you wondering why the hell you entered the jungle in the first place. The next thing you know, you're cowering in the corner of the club muttering to your drink like Tom Hanks talking to Wilson in *Cast Away*.

There is another jungle that contains the same defeating conditions; a Las Vegas casino. Everything from the lavish carpet designs to the

chime of the slot machines, the temperature of the
A/C and the lack of windows is all strategically laid
out to keep you in a trance, gambling and blowing
money fast. There's no coincidence that the house
always wins and most gamblers find it impossible to
quit while they're ahead. It's the ways of the casino.
They spend millions of dollars researching layouts
and their psychological effects on a gambler's
psyche. Their ploy manipulates your mind and
keeps you focused on the pipe dream of winning
big, while at the same time distracting you from the
fact that the odds are heavily stacked against you.
Blackjack, craps, the money wheel, poker, roulette,
etc., the traps are endless. And you can't forget the
ever popular, yet sinister slot machines. The odds of
winning at slot machines are daunting, but gamblers
still pull that handle with foolish optimism.

Even with all the mind-boggling amounts of
money that casinos spend on those tactics, they still
can't compete with human nature. Your most
primal and carnal instincts will always toy with you,
causing you to be hypnotized over an hourglass
figure. Not even the comps given by a casino host
can compare with the comps given in VIP. The fact
is that slot machines and card dealers are stationary
predators. They don't overly solicit your
participation. The trap is set and it's only a matter
of time before you take the bait. However, they
don't walk up to you with a perfect set of fake
breasts, wearing fishnets, clear stilettos, and

whispering those familiar words. "Hey handsome, do you want a dance?" You'll never see a card dealer give a player a winning neck massage or make their butt cheeks clap to grab their attention. Good luck trying to find a pit boss that's willing to sit on a gambler's lap and seductively explain to them the benefits of playing craps.

This jungle is different. It has ways to target your mind, body, and soul of your bank account. It's filled with all types of predators that will devour anything that sits at the tip rail or tries to hide in the dark corners of the club. The stark reality is that you are the prey and you must be situationally aware of the countless ways that you are under attack. Make no mistake, everything here is against you; the cover charge (unless you're military), the astronomical ATM fees, the pricey drinks, and the unfair expectations of making it rain like there's no tomorrow. All this is before tackling the Eternal Patron Dilemma of choosing the right stripper to experience a lap dance that's worth the price. There's the occasional Bird Dog, the overzealous bouncer that can't wait to open the curtain and interrupt your extracurricular activity.

There are the absurd VIP prices, the expensive bottle service, and the overall belief that you should tip regardless of the level of customer service. According to most clubs, the customer is never right. Psychologically, you must be prepared for stripper gamesmanship, the mental and physical chess match that strippers play with patrons. You also have to be ready to maneuver around club rules that are set in place to stymie your inner savage.

In the jungle, you can and will be ambushed from all angles. You must watch your back as well as your front. Strippers aren't the only ones sizing you up, and judging you by your wardrobe (shoes, watch, jewelry, and brand names), wondering if your pockets are loaded. Waitresses and bartenders can also be dangerous, yet unassuming beasts of prey who only want to serve those that they can take advantage of. Often they are more attractive than the strippers themselves. You might find yourself making return visits just to check on her relationship status while ordering watered-down vodka cranberries.

Thinking that you can simply stroll into a club and assume your position, as the King of the Jungle will quickly prove you the village idiot. The truth is that there is no crown.

It is time to clear up a common misconception: lions don't live in the jungle, and actually the lion is not the king at all. In nature, everything depends on circumstance—the situation. If a lion is roaming the savanna and encounters a group of hyenas, that lion will retreat with his tail between its legs. The same thing will happen when it encounters a herd of wildebeests. Lions will also wisely avoid snakes; one spray of venom from a cobra can blind a lion instantly. Even killer bees will have a lion running for its life. You can't forget about the mischievous nature of baboons; they love to hang in trees and urinate directly into a lion's face —that's quite embarrassing. You also have to watch out for other lions that are willing to fight for their territory. Animal references aside, you can see how a gentlemen's club is no different from this wild environment.

SURVIVOR NOTE

To survive this jungle, you must first be conscious of your position within it, and the pitfalls that are lurking around every corner. Protect your ego and your manhood amid this sexual habitat which seeks to drain your wallet and soul; threatening to send you home with a severe case of blue balls, thirst, and starvation, not to mention lost friends; George, Andrew, and Benjamin.

LAW
2

ALWAYS PLAN YOUR
ENTRANCE AND EXIT

For most patrons, planning a trip to the jungle is a foreign concept. Typically, one plans a road trip, but who *plans* a night of debauchery? The common misbelief is that making a trip to the jungle is best as a spur-of-the-moment decision, an uncontrived excursion driven by the sudden desire to gaze at T and A. Foolish patrons presume that an unplanned trip will ultimately end with a classic story and a happy ending. Waking up from a two-day hangover, vaguely recalling how you somehow ended up at a local strip club and miraculously found your way home can be the stuff of legendary tales.

The true survivor understands that certain

misadventures bring unnecessary drama, an exhaustion of resources and real consequences. Every patron needs to understand that organizing and mapping out a strategy to get you from point A to point B is the most effective way to focus on the bottom line—and that's flirting with strippers and not flirting with disaster. Getting lost on the way to the club, misplacing your wallet and car keys, running out of gas, puking up your pre-game drinks, and risking a DUI are only humorous on the big screen. There's nothing honorable about getting hammered and jumping behind the wheel to catch 2 for 1 specials. Getting a VIP seat in a sober tank is not part of the plan. But you only live once, right? Many are too familiar with the temptation of surrendering to their animal instincts. Although there are always exceptions to rules, and in theory, an unforgettable time can happen without a script. When it comes to surviving a gentlemen's club, two things require clear and concise planning—your entrance and exit.

This law is about maturity, efficiency, and being smart. The first step is to do extensive research before making your excursion. It's all part of planning. Of course, one can check for general information on the club's social media accounts. However, there are exclusive websites and forums that give detailed reviews on every jungle—the location, prices, rules of engagement, and the type of predators. You will find stories of survival from a community of veterans that will tell you first-hand that this is not a game. Another option, if you're lucky enough to have one, is to consult with your Mole. She may have priceless intel that can help you with your travel arrangements.

Once you're familiar with a jungle and its predators, then you can ask yourself more specific questions. Who's on the roll call? Why is your Favorite not cooperating? Who's the Tiger that just flew in from New York? Did my go-to club just turn into an Air Dance club? All the fun, unpredictable, spur-of-the-moment challenges should only happen inside the jungle. Dealing with the chaos inside is more than enough to keep your mind occupied and your hands full. That's where you stay on your toes and watch out for booby traps—reading between the lies, avoiding the Vultures, Piranhas, and ducking from rainstorms.

SCENE I

Out of the blue, you receive a phone call from a trusted confidant, "You need to check out _____." Before a smirk can appear on your face, your confidant hangs up abruptly as if avoiding a wiretap. You repeat the name of the jungle in your head, and that's when the questions pop up. Now it's time to plan.

Will this be a solo mission? A solo creep is ideal. You control your destiny. Or will you be part of an entourage? Is each member ready for survival, or are you bringing innocent bystanders to the jungle to get slaughtered? It's vital that everyone knows the laws. There's nothing worse than planning a trip to the jungle with a friend who deep down inside has issues with the strip club game. All you'll hear is complaints and rants.

As far as time, how many hours are you and your friends putting in? It is damn near impossible to make plans inside the club. Once a member of your entourage is caught in the clutches of a predator, and you can't wait to leave—you better get ready to take a nap in your chair, buy an overpriced energy drink, and hope that he's not the designated driver. Speaking of which, are you catching a taxi or contacting Uber or Lyft? That's another decision that should be made before entering. Don't forget that if you need to use Uber or Lyft—they don't take cash, so avoid getting a hold placed on your card for irregular activity. Those high mileage lap dances add up quickly. Also, make sure you have enough battery power left on your phone. Both companies work with mobile apps and you can't book a driver on zero percent.

If you're driving, do you know the area and the surrounding places? Where are the nearby gas stations? Where do the cops hang out? You can't just rely on GPS and Google Maps. Technology won't tell you if you're in the wrong neighborhood. Most establishments are located on the outskirts of civilization—hidden from suburbia, tucked away in urban areas and isolated from traffic—the type of buildings that belong to a ghost town. Again, do your research.

Will you be buying rounds of drinks? Are you getting a VIP table? While some predators enjoy a beer, most never order the cheapest drink on the menu. Rather, on your dime, they like to indulge in cocktails. If you want to "turn up," order a bottle of Hennessy. Before you know it, you're stumbling out of the jungle wasted. Even before you enter, you need a plan of how you will return safely to your destination. Survival should only be a concern *inside* the club. You shouldn't be concerned with surviving the ride home.

SCENE II

You're enjoying the companionship of a sexy stripper. She's fun, down-to-earth, and stunningly beautiful. The lap dances are intense, it's getting sweaty, and the flirting matches the heat in the booth. Her attitude and aggressiveness surprise you, but you're smart enough to recognize that you're in the presence of a Tiger, so you just hold on to her tail for dear life. In your mind, you would love to ask for her phone number, but you resist and play it cool. Although, you will make sure you get her schedule for future visits. Relying on the club's roll call is too risky—Tigers aren't that easy to capture.

It's almost the last call, and she leans in and says, "I'm hungry." You're a bit skeptical, but you quickly realize that this is a small window and you reply, "Let's grab something to eat?"

She answers, "Cool, give me your number… so where are we going?"

This is not the time to look at Yelp reviews or nudge the patron next to you who's busy getting a lap dance. You certainly don't want to start googling places to eat like a rookie. Even though you're surprised that she's willing to meet outside the jungle, you don't want to give her that impression. You always want to be ready for anything. So where are you two going? Do you already know a good spot? What type of food? Is it in the vicinity? When do they close? This apex predator lives in the moment, and there's no way in hell she's taking a rain check. Timing is everything.

What if you're the designated driver? Are you going alone or is your entourage coming along? What's your plan? Nothing screams immaturity like bringing your strip club buddies on a late night meet with a stripper—put them in an Uber or Lyft.

Never answer these questions on the fly. Winging it is a sure way to lose before you even start. Your approach should be businesslike, not amateur. Only rookies embrace immaturity and reckless behavior. Understand the importance of thorough planning and the necessary preparation needed to enter an environment that will provide all the spontaneity and excitement.

SURVIVOR NOTE

Whether you have to gather the troops, do your research on a new jungle or make a solo trip to your favorite spot, your entrance and exit to the jungle should be smooth and easy—no nonsense and no distractions.

LAW
3

CHECK YOUR JEALOUSY
AT THE DOOR

In the competitive jungle, your emotional
state is tested at every step. Throw in a heavy mix of
alcohol, testosterone, and sexual tension, and you
have just stumbled into the lion's den. Make no
mistake, this is the ultimate *snooze, you lose*
environment where emotions run high and
opposition is ruthless—it's every man for himself;
money talks, and there are times when your money
won't talk loud enough. All it takes is one quick
glance at the pole work on stage, and all of a
sudden, Genavie, the stripper sitting next to you is
snatched up and taken for some lap dance fun. But
don't get bitter, the patron has a clear agenda and
it's the stripper's job to follow the money and be an

opportunist. Depending on that patron's bank account, you could be looking at a temporary loss or a full-stage hostage situation. If she happens to get swallowed up by a Whale, a patron who has the deep pockets to keep her in VIP for hours on end, just plan on finding a new target for the evening.

Even if you reserve a bottle service table, a certain celebrity can make a surprise appearance and get you booted quicker than a raincoater wearing a stained black trenchcoat.

It's all part of the capitalistic nature of the jungle. Only the strong survive. If you lose perspective, friendly competition can trigger a salty emotion that is counterproductive to your agenda: jealously.

Now, it's a no-brainer that if you're having a shitty day, it will behoove you not to bring that anger and grumpiness into the jungle. The staff, strippers, and your fellow patrons will appreciate it dearly. There is nothing more deplorable than a patron who wants to spend his time bickering with strippers and getting into a scuffle with patrons. On the other hand, just because you're in a social environment where predators play with your emotions, doesn't mean that you need to combat their tactics by being emotionless. This law is about the strip club game, not the pimp game—where it's a prerequisite to have ice water running through your veins and a heart colder than a polar bear's toenails. It's also the wrong place to be acting like you're the King of the Jungle and that you're above every interaction. Being reluctant to engage and play the game is pointless. You're already dealing with an actress, so there's no need for you to play a role. It is best you live in the moment, and it's okay to wear your emotions on your sleeve, but don't catch feelings (the L-word). That can never happen!

You must understand that most predators can work with a variety of emotions, and that's why most are a part-time therapist. Experiencing loneliness? A girl-next-door type can give you companionship, a shoulder to cry on, and an impromptu therapy session on a velvet couch. Feeling sadness? A high-energy lioness can lift your spirits and much more. Are you a rookie full of nervousness and fear? A MILF with big breasts can nurture you and make you feel right at home. But jealousy is one emotion that even the most experienced stripper can't handle. It is a forbidden topic among patrons; no one wants to admit to feeling inadequate and mentally helpless in a fantasyland. Falling victim to this state of mind is utterly embarrassing and a crushing blow to one's ego. Jealousy is problematic and inside the jungle that negative energy can permeate like cheap cologne. It leads to irrational behavior that clouds your vision, ruins the mood, and makes money-hungry strippers cringe and run the other way.

Jealousy eats away at you like flesh-eating disease. You start to get disoriented and forget that it doesn't matter how much money you have in your pocket compared to other patrons, it's all about how you maximize *your* resources: time and money. There are more than enough g-strings to go around, and every patron can pursue the same goal of getting a lap dance that's worth the price.

But that gets lost somehow when jealousy infiltrates your bloodstream and you start to be possessive and intrusive to the point of becoming the stereotypical ex-boyfriend of a stripper. You know, the one who questioned her every move and didn't respect her hustle. Instead of having a good time, and going with the flow, now you're just an instant buzzkill and a square who is not hip to the game. You're unaware that your stare is a little too long, your questions cross the line, and your attention is focused on the next man's moves—it's a pathetic sight.

There are a lot of emotions, but jealousy is deadly because it awakens all your insecurities. Even envy has its place in the jungle, although that flow of emotion should come and go quicker than a tequila shot. Envy and jealousy come from the same place, but with a healthy outlook, envy can be controlled and transformed into a positive tool. An adrenaline rush of envy will remind you to stop being a spectator, put down the binoculars, and endorse the hierarchy of needs. If you're sitting quietly and you see a patron leaving VIP with two sexy strippers, and he's unable to conceal his devilish smirk, envy will have you wondering what type of fun he had behind the curtain and why you are still stuck in your chair. Or, if a baller is creating a major rainstorm and you find yourself running for shelter, escaping the downpour of dollar bills, envy will have you imagining yourself holding 10 bands and showering strippers with reckless abandon. Hopefully, you're more economical with your money, but the point is that it's understandable to admire having that type of spending power that will attract the most vicious predators. That quick dose of envy will have you saving up money and eager to enter the jungle to stake your territory.

But jealousy will have you violating the hierarchy of needs in the most disturbing way. Rather than enjoying the twerk show on stage, jealousy will have you sitting at the tip rail ranting about how tipping is beneath your strip club standards. Jealousy will have you secretly badmouthing strippers that are performing a dance at the neighboring table while you and your friends wallow in boredom at yours. Instead of flirting and pursuing a lap dance with the newly arrived Tiger from Houston, you'll be too busy trying to eavesdrop on a conversation between your Favorite and a thirsty patron. You become a proud hater, a bitter visitor who feels insecure about their place and ranking in the jungle.

A law-abiding patron always maintains his composure and never results to pettiness. Getting caught up in jealousy is for the rookies.

SURVIVOR NOTE

Keeping a healthy control of your emotions is vital. You must embrace the moment and be responsive to every encounter. Recognize that the energy you bring into the jungle can attract or repel predators, and jealousy by far is the most toxic; ensure that you check it at the door.

LAW
4

CASH RULES, CREDIT CARDS
ARE FOR FOOLS

There is one golden rule that absolutely
applies throughout the liveliness of the jungle:

He who has the cash rules.

A stripper will be the first one to tell you that
money talks and bullshit walks, and she's referring to
the numerous nicknames: dough, bread, cheddar,
dead presidents, moolah, and the list goes on and
on. All these colorful terms let you know there's only
one thing on her mind: cash.

Cash rules everything around the jungle.
There are no freebies in this money pit. You can't
get the most "bang for your buck" without a buck—

period! Having a brick of cash is like holding the conch in the movie *Lord of the Flies*—instantly, you have power and respect, and you also have to watch your back.

When it comes to doing business, cash is the gold standard. It's like the sun, stimulating life for all living things in the ecosystem—predators, waitresses, bartenders, DJs, managers, security, valet, massage girls, and patrons; they all exist because of the power of cash. This is why cash is the first link in the basic strip club food chain.

CASH → PATRON → BARTENDER → WAITRESS → STRIPPER

Fig. 1. Basic Strip Club Food Chain

If you enter a club that forces you to use vouchers or chips, a generic form of legal tender—proceed with caution. Nothing kills incentive and a hustler's ambition like holding a $20 voucher. Yes, indeed it does have value, but cash brings out their predatory instinct to hunt and prolong the encounter.

There's a reason why making it rain with cash is such a natural attraction. The power of cash fluttering in the air, raining down and making the jungle greener is captivating to the eye. Who makes it rain with vouchers? No one. You can take your chances with tossing your chips on the main stage, but that's a risk that most veterans wisely avoid.

Absolutely nothing makes a predator's eyes widen like the sight of a nice stack of bricks. You can see the dollar signs in their eyes. That's why some patrons purposely display a huge amount of cash just for show; it's the classic bait and switch technique. They'll sit at a VIP table and make sure that the predators see the bricks of cash, giving the illusion that they will spend it. However, they only toss out a couple of dollars like a handful of birdseed to a few pigeons. It's an effective strategy. Eventually, predators will flock to see the cash— mission accomplished.

Although the bait and switch is not advised because trickery is not necessary to survive, it is understood as a strategic move that can lure in thirsty predators. That's the visual power of cash. If flaunted, it can make any patron a visible target for the money-hungry. The club can be pitch black, but once you flash a few dollars, predators will turn on their night vision and spot you from across the room in a matter of seconds. Just make sure that you can handle the attack from apex predators who know how to turn you into an ATM.

Most of the time, you can be your own worst enemy. It all depends on what type of strip club accountant you want to be. A professional accountant knows exactly where every dollar goes and its purpose. They can calculate and categorize every cash expense to ensure that sound economic decisions are being made. Or you can be your own shady accountant turning a blind eye to overspending, and disregarding your petty cash fund.

Therein lies the intrinsic benefit of holding cold, hard cash. It allows you to see your budget right in your hands. Do you have enough to cover drinks, tips, and lap dances? You're looking right at your spending limit. You don't have to worry about your personal bank placing a hold on what's already nicely stacked in one dollar bills. You are in charge of what is considered irregular activity. There are no hidden fees that can sneak up on you out of nowhere. It forces you to feel the cash leaving your fingertips, the adrenaline rush as your heart skips a beat with every loss, and your mind ponders; Are you being foolish or economical? Are you choosing wisely or aimlessly? Those are questions that patrons must ask themselves when dealing with cash.

He who uses the credit card is a fool.

It's just too problematic, and rarely does one stick to the budget. This outlook may seem harsh and rigid, but unless you're a Sugar Daddy with an unlimited budget, or you can exercise military discipline, it is far too easy to lose track of your spending when using a credit card. You also have to worry about the potential evidence left on your credit-card statement that you were in the jungle spending $400 on extracurricular activity. Unfortunately, not every jungle has discreet billing. There's also the unreasonable club fee that comes with making a cash advance. But then again, if you're receiving a cash advance, surely those lap dances must be hotter than hell or your planning skills are inept. Even though those issues are minor, the real shenanigans creep up when alcohol takes over the party.

As soon as they swipe your card, that balance is under severe attack, and all it takes is one foolish move to blow up your proposed budget for the evening. The next thing you know, you're staring at the bill wondering who ordered all those tequila shots. You'll also be questioning the multiple service charges that will appear out of nowhere.

Be honest. Who wants to be responsible for keeping track of the quantity of drinks and their prices, let alone the names of the Piranhas that will attack your table? They will come ready to swallow up your bottles and add in their pricey drink request. Piranhas know how to apply the right amount of pressure to your ego and take a big bite out of your account balance—an open tab translates to open season!

No matter how much Piranhas try to seduce you, do not use your credit card to purchase lap dance coupons. You'll end up paying far more than the typical lap dance charge—thanks to the unnecessary convenience fee.

Whether you're buying a couple of rounds or enjoying the perks of VIP, once you're tipsy, you can forget about trying to calculate the bill. You'd rather count how many times your Favorite can make it clap. The drinks are flowing, the music is blasting, and the jungle has you in its clutches. Your credit card is out of sight and out of mind. Overspending becomes inevitable. On the other hand, you can be drunk and still be a decent accountant when you're fumbling through crumpled up dollar bills.

You also have to watch out for what is called "the honest mistake," which you know is no mistake at all! That's when a sexy waitress mysteriously adds a couple of drinks and a tip to the bill. She takes advantage of the party atmosphere and makes a harmless mistake in hope that you might overlook it. It can happen at any gentlemen's club, although foreign locations seem to embrace this scam. The main reason this shady practice is effective is that it's an indirect shaming technique. It preys on the weakest of patrons who want to avoid a confrontation at all costs. If you're that type of strip club goer, be on alert. When you're in the middle of the jungle arguing over a bill, guess who's shamed into looking like the loser in the scenario? You guessed it. Even if you are right, your reputation within the jungle and with its predators will be on display for everyone to see. Now you're on the main stage and whatever you do, make sure that you don't raise your voice to the waitress; it's never a good look. All of sudden, the security is walking over, and now the manager is on his way. You look around for moral support, but all your friends are drunk and occupied with their own survival. The Piranhas have since gone and attacked another VIP table. You're trying your best to explain what's wrong with the bill to an audience of blank faces. The waitress now has the audacity to act like you're wasting her precious time. From afar, it looks like you partied too hard and ran out of funds. It's at that very moment that you realize you made an honest mistake. You just learned that using a credit card was a foolish idea.

SURVIVOR NOTE

Cash is king and working with cash is the best way to eliminate potential shenanigans and unjustified expenses. Always keep things simple and stick to the golden rule.

LAW
5

READ BETWEEN THE LIES

Is a stripper supposed to tell you facts about her life? Is she not supposed to flatter your ego and play with your emotions? She is playing a leading role in your strip club fantasy, right?

The only way to come to grips with the harsh reality of stripper gamesmanship is to deal with the fact that strippers tell beautiful lies.

Truth is beautiful, without doubt. But so are lies.

—Ralph Waldo Emerson

For strippers, it's not about telling you the truth; it's about telling you what you want to hear. In essence, strippers are beautiful liars and most times, patrons love the lies.

Even though some lies will be so blatant that they can rival a stand-up comedy routine—like the stripper who promises you the most mind-blowing lap dances. But in reality, she's a Bunny Rabbit who cringes at the very thought of a touch. Her reputation as a Professional Air Dancer is common knowledge throughout the jungle. Or the predator with the sinister smile who claims that you're the sexiest man she's ever met. Never mind the fact that she tells that to every single patron who walks in the door. Some lies will be mind-boggling, like the predator who acts like you two have never met. She happily introduces herself with a new stage name. Somehow, she forgot about all the money that you blew last week on bottles and terrible lap dances.

Despite the ridiculousness, lies do come with the territory. Think of them as a defense mechanism. By the very nature of the job, strippers should be protective of their personal lives and be intent on keeping things on the surface. Thus, the elaborate world of stage names and alter egos (Foxy, Honey, Juicy, Feisty, etc.). Not every patron has a healthy outlook on the jungle, and unfortunately, there is a fair amount of stalkers hiding in the bushes. In a matter of three minutes, a high mileage lap dance can turn an eager patron into an obsessive client. You know, the guy who's dying to get to know the "real her."

Strippers also have to protect themselves

from jealous girlfriends and wives that would love to start a catfight with their so-called nemesis. If only they could find out a government name and a residence. They may inspect her social media accounts for weeks, and months to no avail. All they'll find is thirsty followers, thousands of selfies, and twerk videos. #ThirstTraps.

Those brief scenarios are the very reason why generic strip club conversation is cliché and superficial but still customary. The exchange usually flows in this order:

What's your name?
Where are you from?
Would you like a lap dance?

Of course, there are variations to this chitchat—add in flattery, a timely compliment, and an awkward stare—but the endgame is always the same. Her objective isn't to deceive you. She's playing within the rules of engagement and she has a clear agenda—and so do you. She just wants to have a flirty conversation that tickles your fancy and targets your pockets. At the same time, making you an open book, while all you get from her is her cliff notes.

As the conversation flows and touches on various topics, the key is to read between the lies and pick up on information that can benefit your agenda.

Even with a club persona and a stage name, strippers are still human. They have a conscience, a strong desire for realness and honest motives. If you listen carefully, little truths will creep out like the animal sounds of the jungle—consider them **trigger words.** These words signify a certain level of hustle and a predatory mind-set.

This skill will take an open ear and keen awareness. You're already accustomed to hearing about the stripper who's paying her way through nursing school or the newbie who's juggling classes at the local city college. There's also the sob story of the stripper whose car broke down, and she needs to make a ton of money, asap. Well, unless you are submitting an application for Sugar Daddy status, hoping to be a sponsor, her aspirations and financial hardships are only good for small talk. They are just beautiful lies told to show you her ambitious side or her burdens, but they mean little in the midst of the jungle. You already know she's on the hustle.

What about her relationship status? It doesn't matter if she has a boyfriend, girlfriend, or a husband. Although a stripper with a ring may quickly highlight her breadwinner status, the only relationship that matters is the one inside the jungle. Don't get excited if she tells you she's single. She knows it will make her look more attainable. Most times, it's just a beautiful lie told to get in touch with your *singles*! That's her *real* relationship status. As far as dating, the less you know in that department, the better.

So what are the trigger words? As you read between the lies, here are a few **words** that will give you a true indication of what type of predator you're dealing with.

Travel. Any predator that travels to Vegas or any other states outside her local jungle is about her money. She's also about the adventure, and living in the fast lane. She's on the money chase, and there's absolutely nothing wrong with that. Travelers are far from naive. They welcome a patron that wants to maximize their dollars—they can relate—take advantage of this truth. This information can also come in handy if you can be creative and timely. It's always good to have a friend when you're traveling, especially one in her profession. True go-getters have a favorite airline, and they're addicted to earning frequent flyer miles. Their calendars are booked with upcoming events: Super Bowl, NBA All-Star Weekend, Daytona 500, Final Four, and both political conventions. Wherever the money flows, they will be there hunting for prey. You can be right there enjoying the festivities. Whether she's traveling solo or most likely in a stripper entourage, there's nothing like moving the strip club experience to a new location. Naturally, the traveler is ready to let her guard down and eager for a good time. That's where you come in.

Bachelor Parties. One thing about predators that perform at bachelor parties is that they are professional and they respect the code of silence. And they love to party. The average predator stays far away from these alcohol induced rituals. But this wild animal is only afraid of counterfeit money. Given that she's used to entertaining a rowdy bunch of bachelors, she has no problem giving you a memorable lap dance—you're light work. It's up to you to capitalize on this truth. She is also a good resource in times of playful party planning. Plus, if you're the groom to be, wouldn't you rather get blindfolded and spanked by a stripper that you already know?

Home (Main) Club. These words will creep out when you're trying to inquire about her schedule and whereabouts. This truth is about accessibility. Predators with a home club are loyal and more likely to stick to the rules. They're thoroughly invested in their club's brand, and that's a signal for you to make a long-term investment. Like (Spearmint) rhinos, they're not hard to find. They're always at the same club, making it easy for you to pinpoint their exact location and implement a strategic plan that caters to your agenda. For example, if you happen to be given a fake phone number by a stripper with a home club, you can happily return and find the culprit. What proceeds after that is up to you, but you get the point!

Works At More Than One Club. If a predator doesn't have a home club and she works at more than one, just know that you spotted the leopard of the stripper kingdom. This truth is about elusiveness. Although you may get a glimpse of her rosettes (tattoos), it's difficult to capture a predator who is not tied down to a local club. You're dealing with a short-term investment and you better have fun while you can. A leopard is always on the run, chasing the money. She can adapt to any environment, and there's no telling what jungle she'll be at next. On Monday, she's at a local topless bar, and then on Thursday, she's across town at an all-nude spot, showing off her fur. You can forget about requesting a real-time, roll call and seeing if she's working for the night. She's not even loyal to a stage name. You might catch her on stage as Jazmin, and then two days later she's on the scene as Sabrina.

Weed. First off, no predator who's serious about smoking weed would ever lie about smoking weed. The typical stripper lifestyle affords her the time and space to indulge in all things cannabis. In fact, some girls start stripping just to support their marijuana addiction. And you thought money was the only green thing they were after. The weed smoker is the least judgmental, least temperamental, and most carefree predator in the jungle. She just wants to make money, give a mesmerizing lap dance and chill. She knows why you're there and has no interest in judging you and your agenda. This type of predator is exactly what you need—speak freely. It's also fair to assume that considering her networking skills; she can always find the *good* stuff. She is a proud member of a culture that stays high. If weed is your thing, there are several ways to take advantage of this information. You never know, she might end up being your plug.

Kids. A predator would never lie about having kids. If you do encounter one that would stoop so low for the sake of the almighty dollar, get away as fast as you can; she's a certified psycho, and the jungle has rendered her insane. Otherwise, this truth quickly highlights her tenured position in the strip game. She's a stable fixture on Cutthroat Island. The chances of her executing on an exit strategy are slim to none. From your survival standpoint, this is a positive. This translates to a consistent work ethic, commitment to her profession, and a predatory attitude. More importantly, she is a sound investment. Once this lioness informs you of her pride, you'll know instantly she respects the hard-earned dollar. As stated in Law 12, Embrace The MILF; she is all about providing excellent customer service because she is honest about her position in the jungle.

These are just a few trigger words that can be used strategically to enhance your strip club experience. It is up you to listen intently, and read between the lies.

SURVIVOR NOTE

Once you come to the realization that strippers tell beautiful lies, the key is to listen closely to their words and pick up on little truths that will eventually creep out. Most information expressed is not valuable and only intended to butter you up for an easy kill. But there are certain trigger words that can be used to strategically enhance your strip club experience and overall agenda.

LAW
6

ALWAYS TIP WITH PURPOSE

When it comes to the dos and don'ts of
tipping, every inhabitant of the jungle has a biased
opinion. Given the different degrees of self-interest,
it's important not to place every opinion in the same
tip jar. You must first understand that tipping is an
investment. Not only are you giving your precious
time, but you are also investing your dollars into the
overall strip club experience. With that economic
outlook in mind, always tip with purpose. Attached
with every single dollar, is your agenda and the
expectation of return. The return on your
investment can be as immediate as a kiss on the
cheek, prompt cocktail service, or it can yield
dividends in the future like a Bird Dog turning a
blind-eye to your savagery in VIP.

Now, of course, waitresses, bartenders, restroom attendants, massage girls, DJs, security, and valet all embrace the kind gesture. In fact, they need tips to survive. It should also come as no surprise that predators are the biggest advocates of tipping and DJs are their most vocal supporters.

But what about the tipper's opinion?

For patrons, tipping is a dicey topic to discuss. Most lack the bravery to take a stand and talk about the dos and don'ts. It's easy to go with the flow and succumb to the pressure applied by strippers. They love to remind you that they're independent contractors without benefits, and someone has to pay the club's stage fee and tip out. Therefore they will use whatever tactic available to promote their agenda, which is to keep you in a daze and encourage frivolous tipping. That's why you'll never hear a stripper take a strong stance against making it rain. They all love the green carpet treatment.

As far as DJs, every patron is accustomed to their spouted propaganda on the morality and etiquette of tipping. Their agenda is loud and clear. They will say whatever funny catchphrase there is that will keep you "tippin' for the strippin'." They won't hesitate to tell you "this is pay-per-view gentlemen and these ladies make their livin' off what you're givin'."

Amidst all the humor, there are a few questions that you must ask yourself. Should you be taking your cues from strippers and DJs? Is it smart to base your survival on their guidelines? Regardless of how unfavorable the situation, are you obligated to tip?

Make no mistake; this law is not an anti-tipping manifesto. Being a non-tipper is the epitome of tackiness. Within your budget, there should be an allocated amount for tips. If you're sitting at the tip rail, do you need to be advised that tipping is customary? Most veterans will tell you that you should tip a least one dollar per song, no matter how short the tune. If you're feeling sympathetic, you can always give what is called a Mercy Tip. That's when no one is tipping, and you feel sorry for her and offer your mercy. The point is, you don't sit there and tease the lions with imaginary rations, knowing they will approach the bars with their paws out. You feed the lions.

If you have nothing to give, do the strippers and your fellow patrons a favor by keeping that seat open for someone who's ready to invest.

The operative goal is to use your money wisely; value every cent. Upholding the hierarchy of needs takes financial discipline and awareness. Given that you have a limited budget, it is unwise to view tipping as a carefree, ostentatious activity. You have an agenda, so be prudent and orchestrated. Your purpose may be to establish a solid reputation with a potential Favorite. It could be to let a MILF know you're aware of her overlooked qualities. Or it could be used to garner the attention of a beautiful Tiger that you would love to capture and take VIP. Whatever your immediate goal, just make sure you're using your dollars to build stripper equity—designate a target and let the interest mature. Don't get tricked into being a good samaritan, a patron who dishes out money for the sake of promoting equality. Do you think strippers treat every patron equally? Not at all. That's not how the jungle works.

So, should you be tipping the stripper who looks down on you? The one who thinks you're a piece of carcass? The one who thinks customer service skills have no place in the jungle, but still has her claws out? What about the stripper who treats you like a pathetic loser for visiting the club?—talk about biting the hand that feeds you.

What about the stripper that's lifeless and sticks to the wall like a taxidermy trophy? And there's always a Vulture that takes a seat beside you and proceeds to deliver the most self-centered conversation. Then she extends her hand and says, "Are you gonna tip me for my company?"

What is your answer? The answer should be a resounding no!

Give an excuse and keep it moving. If you get chastised and accused of being a cheapskate—or better yet, encounter resistance due to your lawful standards—stand your ground. Let those words roll off your shoulder. Controlling your emotions is key to your survival.

Many of you may be shocked by this stance. You're so used to being shamed into tipping that you've forgotten what is means to have a backbone and a purpose. It is vital to understand this tipping principle:

A dollar saved is a dollar they can earn.

Once strippers and DJs hear the word save, they will automatically be up in arms, but as stated earlier, this is not an endorsement for non-tippers. This principle is about being a smart tipper—a strategic investor. It is better to save the dollar that would otherwise go to an unworthy stripper and give it to one who earns it. Only tip the stripper who understands that your dollars are an investment—not a charitable contribution. Invest in those who respect the strip club game and its universal law of reciprocity.

You give her scratch, and she'll scratch your back.

The real hustlers are professional, customer-centric, and they never look down on you. Do not allow yourself to be guilt tripped into tipping a stripper that feels entitled just because she strapped on her stilettos and plastered her body with glitter. Never reward laziness and a lack of hustle. Do you rejoice when you see a lion in a cage, grumpy and lethargic? Laying there empty with no signs of ambition. The lioness has convinced herself that she is a domesticated cat that can just graze your leg and receive a new can of food. It's a depressing sight, and by tipping this unenthusiastic feline, you are condoning her intolerable behavior.

Always remember that the jungle will regulate itself. The stripper food chain is in continual motion. The strong will always survive, staking their territory, earning their keep, and receiving tips hand over fist. The weak will always look for a handout, being dependent on the DJs coercion and your willingness to yield under pressure. This law acknowledges the power and the position that you possess as the tipper. Do not be ashamed to embrace the brutal, capitalistic ways of the jungle. These hard truths are lost when discussing the dos and don'ts of tipping. To tip without purpose is to go against the very nature of a stripper's predatory nature. A real beast of prey relishes the opportunity to hunt—if they don't make a kill, they don't eat. They should always be on the move, active and far from lackadaisical—predators don't beg, they devour.

That's the hardcore reality that strippers conveniently ignore, and DJs will never announce over the microphone. They don't have any funny lines that will address the real issues about tipping in the jungle. But at the end of the day, only you are responsible for your survival and fulfilling your purpose.

SURVIVOR NOTE

Being charitable is honorable and rewarded in the real world, but in the jungle, your donations are not deductible. You are not some faceless organization giving contributions to a wild animal fund. You are a wise investor, one who tips to support your agenda—one dollar at a time.

LAW
7

TAKE CARE OF YOUR WAITRESS

The waitress is the unassuming predator.
Although her methods are subtle; a safe yet
seductive smile followed with a list of familiar
questions, she is adept at using her allure to her
advantage. Naturally, she's the first one on the
attack, even beating out the overly aggressive
Vulture that loves to ambush patrons. As soon as
you walk in and take a seat, she is right there
waiting with a tray in hand. Just make sure you
order quickly and avoid staring into her eyes. That's
how you fall victim to her allure. She's far from the
monstrous, Medusa of Greek mythology, but if you
stare long enough, you will turn to stone and forget
all about your overall agenda. Next thing you know,

you're trying to find out her work schedule and lurking on all her social media accounts with the desperate hopes of making a connection outside the jungle. She is now the main attraction and the reason why you plan your trips. You've forgotten all about the strippers, and that's a blatant violation of the patron's hierarchy of needs.

This Medusa effect happens daily, and that's because most waitresses are devilishly attractive, often rivaling Tigers and other apex predators. The trap is almost unavoidable, especially if they're wearing semi-stripper attire: fishnets, bodysuits, lingerie, swimsuits, etc. From across the room, you might not be able to tell the difference between a stripper and a waitress. Within seconds, you're sucked into a mind game where you can only look, but you can't touch. Stare too long and you can't help but wonder, instead of margaritas—what if lap dances were on the menu?

Some jungles, like several in New York, promote their waitresses more than their strippers. It's a case of strip club blasphemy, but when you have a line-up of servers that look ten times better than the strippers on the main stage, you can't blame them for resorting to desperate measures. They have an agenda, and you have yours. The reality is, that a lot of aspiring models, actresses, and starving students love the part-time flexibility of being a different type of *server* in the jungle; a server that is socially acceptable and free of stigma.

Everyone knows that at the end of the day, a waitress is a convenient side-job, regardless of the environment. It's also a great excuse for a party animal to get a taste of the strip club life without being fully absorbed by it.

But even if waitresses don't blow you away with their looks, they naturally carry a sex appeal that always sparks intrigue. Waitresses are appropriately nicknamed Jill; the little sister of Jane of the jungle. Whereas Janes are the g-stringed predators who roam their territory and devour everything in sight, Jills possess a prudish quality that attracts every patron; they are the damsels in distress. The fact that they are brave enough to work in the jungle, yet still innocent enough to avoid the temptation of the stripper pole is an instant turn-on. Waitresses are the good girl that have only gone a little bit bad—the much sought-after lady in the streets, but a freak in the sheets.

This magnetic attraction can have a patron making return visits just to check on her relationship status and order expensive cocktails, no matter the quality. He may play it off like he's there to visit a Favorite, but in actuality, he's trying to work an angle on his favorite waitress. While he's buying a cocktail, he's also buying his time. Instead of taking care of her and utilizing her skills, he'd rather put on his shiny armor and rescue her from the trappings of the jungle.

However, a survivor understands the

important role that a waitress plays *within* the jungle. Given the nature of the job, her goal isn't to bring out your inner savage or heighten your survival instincts. There shouldn't be a need to read between the lies when she asks you how dirty you want your martini. For the most part, through customer service, her job is to test your level of gentlemanliness. Unfortunately, the jungle can be harsh on waitresses who encounter unruly and lawless patrons who view their job as menial and inconsequential. Those are the same rookies who see tipping as a gratuitous form of exploitation. What type of patron are you? Do you appreciate what a waitress brings to the table or are you the one who is unaware of the benefits of customer service?

It is imperative to understand the three major reasons for taking care of your waitress:

Ally. A waitress that is well taken care of becomes one of your few allies in the jungle. Making sure that her services are greatly appreciated is an investment that has its perks. Whether it's getting put on her guest list, or receiving your favorite table, she can be your personal strip club concierge. When it's every man for himself, it's only smart to have a little help on your side. And who better than a waitress? Not only can she provide prompt cocktail service, but she can also be the perfect go-between in a crowded jungle of savages. The fact that she's the little sister of Jane, she can infiltrate any circle of predators without being attacked. This access can come in handy, especially when you're dealing with the busyness of the Night-Shift. If you need to send an urgent message to a potential Favorite, she can be your trusted assistant. If you want to send a complimentary tequila shot to your Mole, she can get it done smoothly. A motivated waitress can work the floor, get quick information, and be a reliable lookout; to the point that she can tap you on the shoulder and tell you when you've had too much to drink. A gesture that only a fool would disregard. A loyal ally will show concern for your well-being. And with her, if she happens to make an honest mistake on the bill, it's just that; an honest mistake.

Reputation. Your reputation travels quickly from the front door to the stripper's dressing room. And when you take care of your waitress, she becomes your biggest endorser. Nothing makes a waitress gush like the sight of one of her favorite patrons. Her positive energy will reflect in her five-star service, and it will also spread to her team members. If you happen to creep inside the jungle, and your main waitress is not working, another will be more than happy to provide her skills and maintain a high-level of strip club hospitality. You'll be amazed at how easy a waitress can remember the face of a lawful patron whom she's never serviced. Your presence alone will demand attention and respect. That's the power of reputation. Before you know it, your signature cocktail is already ordered before you take a seat. That type of service doesn't go unnoticed by predators who observe everything out of the corner of their eye. You may never know it, but they're already planning their attack on how to reap the benefits of your gold status.

Rapport. If your waitress ever decides to take the leap and hit the main stage to display her hidden twerk skills, guess who's already one of her favorite patrons? You. Since you've built up a rapport with her as a waitress, you will be one of the first to enjoy the release of her freakier side. Most waitresses that make the transition from ally to stripper, experience anxiety and nervousness; it's quite normal. It's very rare for a newbie to throw on a pair of fishnets and become an apex predator overnight. It takes time to work around patrons who come off as creepy and uncivilized. But with you, she will feel comfortable and relaxed which only translates to a good time. She will be excited to take your relationship to an unexplored territory in the jungle. A location where lap dances are the main item on the menu. Also, keep in mind that a lot of waitresses end up being hostesses and managers. In those positions, they will be on the look-out for patrons who want the five-star treatment, and guess who will be the first in line to receive special attention? You.

The importance of the waitress is highlighted, but beware of the waitress that is more concerned with twerking than providing good customer service. A real waitress knows how to play her position and respect the stripper's apex status in the food chain. She can have fun, but by no means does she want to occupy a job reserved for the true hustlers. But this type of waitress is a parasite that only wants to leech off of stripper's energy and satisfy her need for attention. Deep down inside, she would love to strip, but she's afraid to take the plunge. You can tell by her actions. She can care less about strip club hospitality. Taking your order is the last thing on her mind. She just showed up to swindle tips from thirsty patrons who are gullible for wannabe strippers who can never give a lap dance. Some clubs encourage this behavior to support their bottom line, and it's up to you to see through the facade.

Why do you think some managers throw their waitresses on stage to create the Medusa effect? They know the power of seeing an untouchable waitress do a seductive pole routine. Did you think the balloon dance was a harmless creation? That's when a patron buys a mini-lap dance from a waitress who places a balloon on his lap—a beverage usually comes with the purchase. Managers know that when that balloon pops and she turns around, most patrons are already petrified to stone. But you know better than to stare into their eyes and fall for that trap.

Also, keep an eye out for the waitress's sneaky counterpart: the Startender. She's the go-go dancer in disguise. Bartending is just an excuse for her to twerk on the sideline, and collect tips while avoiding the forbidding stripper pole. She can only fix one or two generic cocktails, exposing her lack of respect for the profession. But her attractiveness allows her the ability to also trigger the Medusa effect. That's why she has the audacity to try to occupy a territory reserved for strippers. In fact, what makes the Startender dangerous is that she believes that she is on the same predatory level as a stripper, and furthermore, a notch above the waitress. Instead of respecting the strip club food chain and playing her primary position, she craves to be the star of the show. Her only concern is having a tip jar full of money, and a green carpet beneath her feet.

Ask her if she has plans on earning a bartender's license and she'll give you an odd look. But make sure you don't stare into her eyes and fall victim to her antics. Once she sends you a flirty message like, "I'm behind the bar tonight… come through." It will only be a matter of time before you stop and stare. Next thing you know, you're in a trance tossing dollars instead of tossing back tequila shots.

SURVIVOR NOTE

A savvy patron respects and appreciates what a true waitress brings to the table. And that's more than just a cocktail and a napkin. Survival aside, the waitress is an essential part of making the strip club experience hospitable to a degree. Make sure she is taken care of, and as a result, she will take care of you.

LAW
8

CHOOSE WISELY: IT'S MORE LAP AND LESS DANCE

STAGE 1: WHO DO YOU CHOOSE?

Once you exclude the wasteful and gratuitous act of making it rain, the easiest way to blow your money is by choosing the *wrong* stripper for a lap dance. This challenge is the most crucial and monetarily volatile decision in the jungle. It's the Eternal Patron Dilemma. Who do you choose?

It's very telling and ironic that your primary pursuit—the coveted lap dance—can also be the source of your pain and suffering. The climb is rigorous and when you're at the top of the pyramid scanning the room for a target, exchanging glares with money-hungry predators, that's when you begin to hear the Jeopardy! theme music.

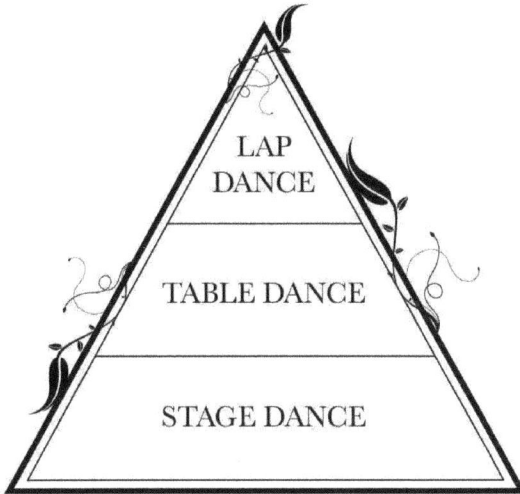

Fig. 1. Patron's Hierarchy of Needs

The following questions appear on your mental screen: Which predator will provide the most "bang for your buck"? Who will take the money and run? Who specializes in giving more lap and less dance?

All the while, reminding yourself that looks are deceiving, and words are misleading. A predator that can twerk, work a pole, and deliver a killer stage dance, doesn't automatically mean she will give *you* a killer lap dance. In the same fashion, the intense eye contact that you get during a mouthwatering table dance gives you no indication that *you* will get a mouthwatering lap dance. Once you deal with these risky factors: ever-changing attitude, thirst level, views on mileage, and stripper experience, you will understand that there is no direct correlation.

What you see is not always what you get.

You have to find out the hard way, and that's by emptying your pockets and rolling the dice. Surviving vicariously through another patron is not an option when visiting the jungle. Considering the fixed price of a lap dance and if you plan to add a tip at your discretion, every decision is a Daily Double.

Most patrons yield under the pressure of having to choose the right one and go off impulse. This decision is called a Blind Lap. When you choose to get a lap dance from a stripper whom you've never seen twerk, booty-shake, perform on stage, or give a lap dance. You blindly roll the dice and hope you come up with mileage. It's a risky move. A lot of predators oversell their dances, and others take their time, only reserving the extracurricular activity for their Regulars. This gamesmanship by predators just adds more complexity to an already tough decision. That's why some patrons just say, "screw it" and survive on this strip club maxim:

The hottest strippers give the worst dances.

This doctrine is strip club gospel to many who firmly believe this is best the way to narrow down the selection. It's common knowledge that 9's and 10's can afford to be spoiled and picky. But even with this philosophy, you can still blow your money on 5's and 6's who appear thirsty and talk a good game. Indeed, the very nature of the jungle is to play with your head. The intensity will bring out the Peeping Tom in some patrons. They'll find themselves in the corner, ogling at a stripper giving a Regular a lap dance. Their inner voyeur is awakened, staring and wondering if she is the one who provides the mileage. Often, patrons take the easy route, relying on recommendations from their fellow counterparts. But that's still a roll of the dice. Valuable intel is priceless, but believe it or not, *chemistry* does play a part when you're one-on-one. Just because a stripper gives one patron a solid lap dance, doesn't guarantee you equal treatment. Given all the challenges, you can now understand why it's called the Eternal Patron Dilemma. And this is why a good number of patrons secretly make it rain and stay at the tip rail all night.

STAGE 2: WHAT IS HER LAP DANCE STYLE?

Once the first song starts, only then can you get an idea of how she likes to treat her prey. This reality is what makes choosing such a dilemma.

Everything happens on the clock. In the short span of one song, a lap dance can provide a variety of possibilities, mystery, and anticipation for a happy ending. It can also be a buzzkill, serving you a harsh reminder that you hold little power in the jungle. And this is only the second stage of choosing wisely. Not only do you have to worry about the DJ cutting the songs short, but you also have to watch out for the following lap dance styles. Some are blatant violations to your agenda, while others are very shrewd and strategic ways to give you more dance and less lap.

The Social Lap Dancer. This predator is the social butterfly of the jungle. She is the type to have a conversation with another stripper, patron or staff while giving you a lap dance. Say the wrong words, and she'll start talking about politics. She is easily distracted and loves to waste vital seconds during a song. In fact, she would rather tell you a story than give you a lap dance.

The Taekwondo Lap Dancer. This predator is an expert at using her knees. Instead of giving you more lap, and a little grind, she'd rather keep her distance and use her knees as a weapon. It's an interesting take on physical contact. Whether it's a knee to the stomach or a slight graze to the groin, brace yourself for the intense knee action—things can go either way.

The Shady Accountant Lap Dancer. This predator will take advantage of your drunkenness and add extra dances to the count. Things go well in the beginning, but sooner or later, her true colors will show. She bleeds green and only sees patrons as dollar signs. You're just another number on a long list of victims. Don't learn the hard way, always make sure you're aware of the lap dance count at all times.

The S&M Lap Dancer. This predator loves to inflict pain by aggressively grabbing your head and pulling on your clothes, twisting or biting your nipples, and kneeing you to the groin. She thinks it's cute and fun to be domineering but you never signed up to be a slave. Although you admire her passion for breaking the touch barrier, you never thought about squirming and cringing during your lap dance.

The Rule Enforcer Lap Dancer. Before the first song even starts, this predator is already lecturing you on the rules of the club. What you can do and especially what she won't do! She is the local party pooper—the instant downer. She ruins whatever fantasy is running through your head and snaps you back into the reality that some strippers don't know the game they are playing.

Even with all the stripper antics listed above, there is one lap dance style that strikes fear in every patron: **The Professional Air Dancer.** In normal circumstances, the word air would be welcomed. Air helps give life throughout the planet, but in the jungle, air represents lifelessness. The Air Dance is a no contact lap dance, but this isn't merely about the physical space—the air—between you and a stripper. It also signifies a seismic disconnect, a direct contrast in strip club ideology. The primary goal is to obtain a lap dance that's worth the price. The Professional Air Dancer believes that a patron's desires have no place in her make-believe, burlesque world. She is a prude stuck in the *space* age. She is a disruptive outlier, a Bunny Rabbit prancing around the jungle. That's why it's always a shock to find a Professional Air Dancer dwelling amongst the snakes, Tigers, Vultures and Piranhas. How can it be? How is this possible?

You don't have to be a complete savage of a patron to realize that the worst feeling in the jungle is receiving an Air Dance. The experience is demoralizing, and leaves you deflated. You feel scammed—chewed and spat out—by a Bunny Rabbit of all animals! The ordeal often creates a situation called the Air Dance Ripple Effect. That's when you spend your hard-earned money on an Air Dance, and the impact makes you immediately want to replace that feeling with the adrenaline rush of a high mileage lap dance. You feel compelled to fill that void left by air. Your focus is on erasing that memory at all costs, and that's where the ripple effect begins. Just like a gambler, you start rolling the dice, hoping for that "high." You scan the room, anxiously looking for a target. If you don't choose wisely, you run the chance of getting another Air Dance, losing more money and creating a bigger void that will only cause you to roll the dice again—and then again. Things spiral out of control, until you run out of money and air.

STAGE 3: BE READY FOR STRIPPER GAMESMANSHIP

Once you take into account the shrewd levels of stripper gamesmanship, there's no wonder why some are scared to death to play this strip club version of Jeopardy! The experience can be nightmarish, especially if you're dealing with a jungle that uses vouchers, chips, or a bill acceptor. Part of choosing wisely is recognizing that the ideal establishment to enter is one that works strictly on a cash exchange basis between you and the stripper—no vouchers, no chips, and no machines. This way everything is based on chemistry and the progression of one dance to the next. Although the prices vary per jungle (usually $20 for topless, $40 for full nude), you can buy a lap dance for $20, and if you enjoy it—you can tell her to keep going. If the lap dance is not to your liking, you can cut your losses and move on. In this case, you've only lost $20. This natural flow allows you to gauge her level of hustle and ultimately, you get to see who provides the most "bang for your buck." It also gives the stripper an incentive to deliver a satisfying lap dance that will keep the money flowing. There's no visible timer and no mental time limit to interrupt the moment. On the other hand, if you enter a jungle where you have to determine upfront the number of dances that you want, the situation can get tricky. Whether you're holding a $60 chip or you have to fork over $60 so it can get sucked into a bill acceptor, things can take a dangerous turn when you're one-on-one with a cunning predator.

SCENE I

You found a sexy stripper with a slim-thick body that you want to try out for a lap dance. Not only is this stripper breathtaking, but also her energy and allure are captivating. Routinely, you would start slow, but because this particular jungle uses a bill acceptor, you figure you might as well make it worth it. Buying one dance would be a tease, so you buy three lap dances at $20 a pop. She grabs your hand and takes you to a booth. You give her $60, and she slides the cash into the bill acceptor. With perfect timing, the DJ starts the first song.

The first two lap dances are extreme teases. She gives you a hint of an Air Dance, but just enough touch to get you salivating. But the third song, she turns it up a notch and increases the mileage. All of sudden, the eye contact is more passionate, her hips are swerving as she grabs your shirt for stability. It's on and poppin! Then, abruptly the song ends, but your adrenaline is now simmering. You immediately think to yourself, "Where was that energy on the first two dances?"

If this encounter were based on a cash exchange, you would've told her to keep going and prolong the moment. However, she seductively turns around and says, "Do you want more dances?" That's when you start to hear the Jeopardy! theme music.

Within that short break, the chemistry and momentum begin to fade as she confidently awaits your decision. Time is money in the jungle, and there's a good chance she could be snatched up by another patron, so you decide to buy three more dances. You hand over $60, and she waits for the song to end before sliding the cash into the bill acceptor. Now you're nervous, realizing that you're at her mercy. You already paid up front, and you can only hope for a taste of that last dance. Finally, she slides in the cash, and you sit back with anticipation as the DJ starts the next song. She begins to tease and tease and tease. As each second passes, you're waiting for her to turn it up a notch, but sadly it never happens. The timer hits zero and by your blank expression, she already knows not to ask for another set of dances. She quickly takes off into the darkness of the jungle.

In your eyes, you've just blown $100 on five mediocre dances that you can't get back, no matter how duped you feel. There's no refund and good luck trying to find a customer complaint desk. If you track down a manager, they will gladly laugh in your face and tell you there's no crying in the jungle. These are the defeating conditions that are mentioned in Law 1, Know The Ways Of The Jungle. This reality alone is the reason why some avoid entering a strip club. It has nothing do with not finding strippers visually appealing. Certainly, everyone has a type. For many, it's just hard to feel entertained while you're watching your money floating down the river. Imagine the hundreds of dollars that can be lost in 15-30 minutes in VIP.

That's when you see patrons making that Walk of Shame out of the jungle, and you can just hope and pray that depression doesn't settle in right there in the parking lot.

SURVIVOR NOTE

Choosing a stripper for a lap dance that's worth every penny is no easy task. You must take your time, be observant, and still realize that you're rolling the dice on a decision that provides the biggest loss or the biggest reward.

LAW
9

AVOID THE GRUMPY AND BITTER

As you casually walk through the jungle
observing predators that begin to eye you slowly—
gazing and sizing you up from head-to-toe, you will
quickly notice the strategic movements and
characteristics of each lurking predator. Some may
exhibit a subtle shyness or a bubbly personality. A
few might flash a girl-next-door smile or a
nonchalant glare. But while your eyes wander and
look for a target, there is one stripper that you must
avoid at all costs. Stay far away from the grumpy
and bitter. A combination that is lethal and
venomous. Her infectious energy alone can
desecrate the jungle. Have you ever seen the movie
Predator? Think about the self-destruct timer that was
set at the end of the movie—that's her! And just like

Arnold Schwarzenegger's character, Dutch, you better run for your life.

Keep an eye out for the signs. It can be a "resting bitch face," a blatant shitty attitude, or body language that screams I'd rather be shoe shopping—if only she had a Sugar Daddy, of course. Whatever the signs, maintain your distance and evade whoever is a member of her cranky crew. The best prevention is never to make eye contact and hope she's glued to her cell phone. That's when you look straight ahead and tiptoe past like a stripper who is avoiding a stalker. Immediately, talk to a friendly feline with a welcoming smile and a glowing vibe—mission accomplished. You've avoided a case of yellow fever. But it's not always that easy. She will make a half-hearted attempt at making some money.

SCENE I

Things might look promising in the beginning. A sexy stripper approaches with a reluctant smile accompanied by a curvy body. You like what you see. But once this predator takes a seat and opens her mouth, the complaints and negativity slowly take center stage. "These customers don't tip." "There's no money in this club." "I need to make an extra $200." "Where the ballers at?" "I need someone to make it rain." Although her grumpy words may seem relevant, she's babbling about topics that have nothing to do with your agenda. You certainly didn't pay a cover to hear her gripes and struggles. The plan is to escape reality somewhat—not get slapped in the face with unprofessionalism. But you figure she's just having a bad day. It happens to everyone, especially in the jungle. There could be a variety of reasons why she's feeling grumpy. Maybe it's recent comments from a rude patron, or maybe she's going through some personal issues that you wouldn't dare discuss. It's quite possible that the jungle is experiencing a drought, and every patron knows the difficulties of dealing with thirstiness. Therefore, you take it as harmless chatter and wisely decide to direct your attention towards the activity on the stage, particularly the toned-stripper that's doing a sexy job of air walking on the pole. You want nothing more than a spirited good time and the chance to relieve some stress. And her grumpy attitude is killing the vibe.

Without warning, she brings her attention towards the competition on stage. "She always does that move." "I mean, she's cute and all, but she needs a boob job." "Her outfit is not working." She turns to you with a condescending look, "You like those type of girls, don't you?"

That's when you realize she's not having a rough day. She's been afflicted with bitterness, a condition that for most parts is irreversible. The strip club life has jaded her. It's one thing to have an opinion, but her comments derive from a deep-rooted place of low self-esteem and resentment. Stay calm! You have just spotted the most dangerous predator in the jungle. For a second you were considering asking her for a lap dance, but now you just want to hit the restroom to escape this stripper version of "Debbie Downer." At this point, you'd rather talk to the restroom attendant.

Once bitterness has overtaken a stripper, accept the fact that the damage has been done. She will try her best to play the victim and shame you into being a sponsor, but consider her a lost cause. It can happen to the best in the business. No stripper is immune. In no time, a sexy strut can turn into a lethargic, dragging of the feet. It can be a failed exit strategy or the false impression that stripping was "easy money." It could simply be competing in a stripper food chain that's full of apex predators that battle for every single dollar. Struggling to pay tip out, while watching other strippers receive the green carpet treatment can be frustrating and disheartening. Over time, those feelings fester and grow like a fungus. Sooner or later, one can crack under the constant pressure to make ends meet. Instead of stepping up her game, she will continually blame others for her disposition and lack of prosperity. But please understand that it's not your responsibility to find the source of her disappointment. You're not a House Mom and you're certainly not a member of some wildlife conservation group out to save the severely wounded. It is a complete waste of time and money to mold self-esteem in a jungle. Normally, you're the one on the couch receiving an evaluation from an unaccredited therapist, but now you're feeling like the strip club Dr. Phil—and that's never the goal!

Not only does a grumpy and bitter stripper ruin the fantasy, but if you stick around too long, her miserable attitude will rub off on you. Before you know it, you will start to question why you decided to visit the jungle in the first place. Pursuing a lap dance will seem senseless and childish. To thoroughly enjoy this playground, you must enter with a healthy attitude. This environment is supposed to be a place of relaxation and sexual indulgence. But this deadly predator will have you feeling guilty as if you contributed to her misery. All of a sudden, you're now a conspirator to her bitterness and the reason why she decided to work the pole. You're now responsible for her negative views on the jungle and those who dare to visit. You'll start taking on the sentiments and conservative views of an outsider; the strip club is only a place for deviants and raincoaters.

That's why she is the most dangerous. Her attitude infiltrates your brain, and you become disoriented about your position and purpose in the jungle. You're now off your game, slowly becoming numb to the sight of a perfect body and a positive attitude.

Your only cure is to get a killer lap dance from a predator who specializes in giving heart attacks—that's high mileage and extracurricular activity. But you better hurry up! Her condition spreads like the plague. It's contagious, incurable and everyone knows it. The DJ, waitresses, bartenders, and even the security are aware of her infectiousness. The other predators are far too aware. They try their best to stay away, but that negative vibe doesn't just remain on the main floor; it creeps into the dressing room. Now you know the dirty secret to why some dancers get dressed so quickly and rush out the building—they're getting away from her!

The apex predators who are on top of their game keep their space from this Debbie Downer. They don't want the drama and the negative energy and you shouldn't either.

SURVIVOR NOTE

To have a worthwhile time in the jungle, you must avoid the physical and mental clutches of the grumpy and bitter. Always remember that a stripper with a negative attitude will never give you a positive experience.

LAW
10

BE WARY OF THE VULTURE
AND THE PIRANHA

THE VULTURE

Given the Vulture's one-dimensional
approach and volatile attitude, she won't be hard to
identify. Although she will try her best to
camouflage and blend in with the more calculated
predators, her appetite for a quick kill will always
blow her cover. As soon as you walk into the club
and take a moment to scan for an empty seat, a pair
of eyes will be piercing through your pockets from
across the room. While the other predators observe
and wait for an opening, her mouth is salivating
profusely at the opportunity of a sneak attack.
Suddenly, the Vulture swoops in and takes aim at

your neck. Before your butt can barely touch the seat, she's already picking away at your flesh. "Do you want a lap dance? Come on, let's go have some fun. I'll show you a good time." You just sat down, but from her standpoint, this is where you're most vulnerable. Caught off guard, she's hoping that her mere presence is enough to make you weak at the knees and cough up money like an ATM.

"I just got here…I'm gonna get settled in, but maybe later we can have some fun?"

You expect a smile and a flirty response, but she rolls her eyes and gives you attitude. Before storming off, she mumbles the words, "Why are you here if you don't have any money?"

You're stunned! The first thing that pops into your head is "What the hell was that?" You've only been there for 10 minutes, and you're already labeled a spectator, a patron who simply watches all the activity in the jungle with no plans of getting their hands dirty and spending money.

Or you've just taken a seat away from the main stage. You found a nice spot where you can hide in the shadows and evaluate the talent before easing into the mix of things. You're mentally getting ready, applying on your camouflage face paint, and adjusting your trousers, making sure everything is situated in the right place. All of a sudden, you look to your right, and a Vulture appears out of nowhere like a ghost from strip club past. Her talons (claws) are showing, and before you can even say hello, she's already waved in a partner. They don't even bother asking your name, or what brings you into the jungle. These Vultures are breathing down your neck, demanding tips, ordering food and trying to get tipsy on your tab. They're also selling you the most amazing VIP in strip club history. The typical scripted conversation has been pushed aside for ultimatums and bully tactics. Forget about seduction. The Vulture only drives the hard sell. They want you to believe that if you don't adhere to their needs, something is clearly wrong with you. You're just a piece of carcass, and they're trying to skeletonize you in a matter of minutes. Although you have all the time in the world to choose, you are on their schedule, and the clock is ticking. The scavenger hunt is on—or shall one say, the scavenger hustle is on.

THE PIRANHA

It's critical to understand the difference between a Vulture and a Piranha. While both predators are overly aggressive, the Piranha is more opportunistic and selective. And you don't have to walk into the water to receive a ferocious bite. All you have to do is reserve a VIP table. Unlike the Vulture, the Piranha only attacks in a pack, and they make it a point to avoid the simpletons and rookies on the main floor. They target the larger prey—ballers, bachelor parties, and potential rainmakers who want to make a big splash in the VIP area.

Piranhas love to circle and spot the big fish. They may have completely ignored you in the past or assumed you were a guppy, but as soon as they see you talking to a host or manager about a table, they begin to gather in a shoal formation. You may think you've secured a rest haven in the jungle, but invite the wrong strippers to your table, and you'll definitely be swimming with the Piranhas. To avoid an attack, it's best to ask a couple of newbies who are ready to ingratiate themselves into your festivities. But if you leave an opening, you and your entourage will be eaten alive in a feeding frenzy. These relentless predators will scurry to your table, flashing their razor-sharp teeth and take big bites out of your ego and tab. Piranhas are heartless— don't expect them to remember your name. They just want to know the names of the bottles that are coming to your table. They survive off bottle service; taking shots of tequila and consuming bubbly make up their diet. They'll certainly stir up the waters by putting on an eye-popping twerk show, but once the rain and alcohol dry up—they're gone!

After the assault, the only thing left is a table full of empty bottles, and napkins with fake phone numbers and lipstick prints. It's a bloody massacre.

These scenarios expose the very nature of the Vulture and the Piranha. These strippers prey on the naive and specialize in the ambush attack. When you least expect it, they will strike quick and apply pressure until you buckle and forfeit over your cash. The truth is, they lack the poise to be a real strip club seductress. Their strategy is to take advantage of your wild sex drive. They believe that you have no self-control and presume that your horniness will cloud your ability to be selective. Instead of encouraging a reciprocal relationship, they figure you'll accept any attention that comes your way. In their eyes, you're a pathetic loser that has to spend money to see T and A—so shut up, be happy, and enjoy their company. But you're smarter than that. They fail to realize that there is nothing enjoyable about shamelessly being hustled for everything in your pockets including the lint.

The last thing they want to encounter is a patron who exercises patience. A capable strip club goer who values his money and thinks with his head (the one at the top) is the arch nemesis of the Vulture and the Piranha. Withstanding their vicious attack will certainly get their g-strings in a bunch. Showing discipline and having the audacity to consider your options irritates these predators to their core.

Understand, that you're dealing with the strip club nickel-and-dimers. Most outsiders think patrons are the only ones who have to control their thirst—Vultures and Piranhas have to do the same. Don't believe for one second that they're immune to bouts of desperation. Although thirstiness with the right attitude can be a win-win situation, a Vulture and a Piranha on a warpath for a quick kill will always belittle you and sell you short. A mistake that is very costly for predators. Instead of playing a lead role in a fantasy, they'd rather pressure you into getting one of their lackadaisical $20 lap dances, unaware that you have $500 in your pocket, and you can't wait to blow it on the *right* stripper. Unfortunately for them, that money will be spent on a predator who knows how to work an even exchange.

Their approach also reveals that they have no loyal clientele, and they lack the patience to build one. If a predator doesn't understand the importance of a reliable customer base, then you can't fully expect her to respect the value of a hard-earned dollar.

The nickel-and-dimers conveniently disregard the strip club law of reciprocity. They'd rather settle for a quick scheme—a hit-and-run—an extremely fake conversation, and a "fuck you, pay me" type attitude. Instead of a flirty game of tug-of-war, they prefer a game of surrender.

SURVIVOR NOTE

Whether on the main floor or at a VIP table, who wants to be patted down and fleeced for all their belongings? Always stick with those who go with the flow and know how to play the game of seduction. And be wary of the Vulture and the Piranha who are hell-bent on forcing the issue and bleeding you dry.

LAW
11

CATCH A TIGER BY THE TAIL

There are several types of predators in the
jungle that are ready to attack at any given moment,
but there is only one that combines beauty and
hustle like no other; the Tiger. As soon as you make
eye contact, you will be intimidated by her sex
appeal. Within seconds, you're already wondering if
you've found a new Favorite. You start to think of
clever ways to inform your CF (Current Favorite)
that her time is up and your dollars will be headed
in a different direction. That's the power of her
allure. She is simply too good to be true. The Tiger's
beautiful face alone spawns jealousy throughout the
stripper ecosystem and the dangerous part—she
knows it. Every inhabitant of the jungle worships
and admires her body from head to toe. That's why

management gives her free rein. They don't want her to bounce to another club and enhance their reputation overnight. Predators respect her looks so much; they tolerate her ferocious attitude. It's not that she's incapable of being cordial and sociable—it's quite the contrary—it's just that time is money, and when you're that focused on an exit strategy, one doesn't have the luxury to be concerned about everyone's feelings.

The Tiger stays on the hunt, quick to flash her sharp teeth and battle for supremacy. Tigers are the type that professional athletes and celebrities drool over. They make the best arm candy for those looking for a trophy. Even Sugar Daddies have a tough time locking down this feline. She has options and can afford to be picky with sponsors. Her cell phone is buzzing with guys biding their time for a dinner date. But her focus is on her short-term and long-term goals. Status is a big thing for this go-getter, and she'd rather take the connections over the money because, at the end of her shift, she's a beast when it comes to stacking dollar bills.

Some of the qualities mentioned above like beauty, allure, and the ability to focus are not exclusive to one predator, so how does one know you're in the presence of a Tiger?

TIGER-SPOTTING I

The first sign is when you start to think to

yourself, "She's too pretty to be a stripper." You can't believe for the life of you that she's roaming the jungle. The question keeps popping up in your head, "Why in the hell is she working here?" You start to be judgmental, making assumptions about her childhood, intelligence, and current circumstances. That's when you know you've spotted a Tiger. Your intuition is telling you that something is wrong with this picture. You've become hypnotized by her stripes and powerful aura. Before you fall into the trap of being a simpleton—a Tarzan figure who's trying to save Jane from the dangers of the jungle—recognize the situation and focus on taking advantage of what's in front of you. The Tiger is a rare species. She's sexy, flirty, and ready to grind—mainly because her time in the jungle is limited. She is on the brink of extinction. Her kind doesn't stay around too long. You will have to catch this Tiger by the tail and hold on tight. That's what differentiates a Tiger from the rest of the other predators. Where most fantasize about leaving the jungle, the Tiger has her eyes set on an early retirement date—and she is dead serious. It's almost as if stripping is just an item on her bucket list. She treats it as a side-hustle, a perfect gig to raise seed money for her career, pay off student loans or just a 5-month stretch of stacking enough dollars to buy a BMW—and then she will disappear.

TIGER-SPOTTING II

The second sign is once you take a seat and make an attempt to pick her brain, she can't help but reveal information on her budding career as an actress/model or expound on her entrepreneurial pursuits. But this chat is a bit different from the average stripper conversation. Everything she says is backed up with concrete evidence. If she's ecstatic about an upcoming movie role, she can show you pictures of herself on set. If she's opening up a yoga studio, she can give you the address and even offer a free consultation. If you have a female friend that needs a new hair stylist, she's more than willing to slide you her business information. The point is, she's not stuck in a pipe dream. The Tiger already has one foot out the door. The jungle is a financial stepping-stone and unlike the MILF, she has no desire for being a lifer. She is so adamant about her exit strategy that she won't hesitate to look you in your eyes and tell you her last day. And when she does, do yourself a favor, and believe her.

Once you know you're dealing with a Tiger, make sure you match her aggression. Most patrons cower and hesitate to pursue a lap dance. Many settle for giving her a tip and a compliment. Just like any apex predator, the Tiger can smell fear from across the room. Any sign of weakness and she will quickly step over you and find the next alpha patron. Although she is far from the Vulture and Piranha, she is trying to have fun, and the last thing she wants is a patron who is scared to grab her by the tail. Let her know that you are equally ambitious and ready to enjoy the moment.

Two major qualities make the Tiger the biggest catch in the jungle:

Personality. The Tiger is far from a diva and that alone catches you off guard. You even think to yourself; maybe she was an ugly duckling growing up. Fortunately, for whatever reason, she kept that girl-next-door quality, and that makes her a killer. Usually, the 6's and 7's have that cool, down-to-earth personality that puts you at ease. The 9's and 10's usually let their beauty carry the conversation. But her combination of sexiness and coolness instantly makes her a popular creature in the jungle. She doesn't take herself seriously, and that is why she is revered by many.

Sexuality. The Tiger will never verbally admit it, but stripping allows her an excuse to bring out her hidden sexual side. Instead of going to normal clubs and dealing with the typical routine of turning down guys at the bar, the strip club is the perfect place for her to let loose. Since she won't be stripping for long, the Tiger has no issues with giving high mileage lap dances. That's what makes her such a catch. The Tiger is anti-Air Dance. Her dirty secret is that she is an exhibitionist and a voyeur. The sexual nature of the jungle excites her. She thoroughly enjoys taking care of alpha patrons.

It is wise to appreciate every second spent with a Tiger. Eventually, you will have to let loose of her tail—and that's okay. Take comfort in knowing that you survived a tussle with the biggest feline of them all. Because once she's gone, there will be no trace of her ever working in the jungle—no footprints, no remains, and no fossils. You can try your best to dig up some dirt and find out if she changed clubs or skipped town, but you'll come up with zero intel. She's now a mythical figure to those who were lucky enough to witness her curves up close. Her stage name will be a distant memory like the Bali tiger, an extinct subspecies that was last recorded in the 1930s.

Her transition from the stripper pole to the concrete jungle is seamless. Overnight, she will transform into a different type of feline—one more domesticated, civilized, and docile. You can check her social media accounts and find no indication whatsoever that she can twerk with the best of them. Once in a while, she may post a playful twerk video and give a glimpse of her skills, just to have her followers thirsty and curious.

Where did she learn how to do that?

Still, most of her fan club members will

never jump to the conclusion that she learned all her techniques from the jungle. If they only knew, they could see it in her eyes—the hustle, the aggression, the ambition is right there inside. But now she has shifted that energy to a new game— acting, modeling, hosting, businesswoman—or whatever her new direction, you can never knock her hustle.

SURVIVOR NOTE

If you find a Tiger, hold on tight and enjoy the ride. Her days in the jungle are numbered, but her memory will forever be embedded in your brain —and if you're lucky, you'll be the one to cherish unforgettable moments in VIP with a girl that many would never believe conquered the jungle.

LAW
12

EMBRACE THE MILF

Within the stripper ecosystem, there is one stripper that you must embrace; the MILF. Only a rookie will disregard the importance of this savvy and experienced predator. Given that a jungle is a *visual* playground, the typical patron ethos is rooted in this common misbelief:

The sweeter the eye candy, the better the experience.

But this is far from the truth. A young, drop dead gorgeous stripper with a killer body can carry an inflated ego, a bitter attitude, and the opportunistic appetite of a Piranha; none of those traits translate to a high mileage lap dance, let alone an entertaining experience that's worth every penny.

But without clear perspective, your eyes will fail to recognize the utility of the jungle's number one hard-worker.

The first step is to clarify the meaning of the term MILF. By strip club standards, the traditional definition of MILF demands further explanation. The typical "Mother I'd Like to Fuck" acronym is too general. Honestly, most strippers have kids. In fact, that's typically the reason why most decided to work the pole in the first place; the priority here is not to pass judgment—bills need to be paid, and mouths need to be fed. It is what it is.

The focus is undoubtedly not on young mothers in their 20's with a cute kid and baby daddy issues. The 20-something mothers who have yet to hone their sex appeal and master the art of seduction are not a part of this law. A MILF is an older woman in her dirty 30's and filthy 40's with a kid or a few. It's not just about her age; however, it's mainly about the years she's worked in the strip club game. When it comes to life in the jungle, it's important to note that stripper's age in dog years; 2 years of stripping is the equivalent of 6 years (multiply the year by 3).

A real MILF is a seasoned veteran who has put in 30-plus years. She's danced at multiple clubs and has wiped down many poles. She's learned the ropes at the Spearmint Rhino's and Déjà Vu's. She got her start at clubs that have now either acquired new management or completely shut down. She's done Las Vegas, Miami, Houston, and was accumulating frequent flyer miles before they became a thing.

Work-wise, the MILF is cordial with other predators, but she doesn't have many friends. She's too busy to be looking for a BFF or to be a member of a stripper entourage. Frankly, she has no time for drama in her life; her kids occupy that department.

The MILF is essential to the stripper food chain. She's a cunning predator that helps keep the ecosystem in balance. You have Tigers roaming the jungle, focused on their exit strategies. You have your Piranhas trying to ravage every VIP table and Vultures picking at every simpleton on the main floor. And then you have your typical money-hungry newbies with their unreliable work ethic and single-minded attack mode. The type of stripper that will ask you for a lap dance before even asking your name. On the other hand, the MILF brings stability to the jungle by keeping the focus on customer service minus the inflated ego. She respects the hard-earned dollar and understands the bottom line —patrons want the most "bang for their buck" and she's all about providing the bang! She stays on the lookout for patrons that are willing to appreciate what she brings to the table. The key word is "appreciate." A MILF appreciates a compliment, a good conversation, a tip as well as your time. If you order a MILF a cocktail, she will sit there and finish it without hesitation. She doesn't take anything for granted and given her strenuous position in the jungle; she can't afford to.

Being overly aggressive, bossy, and demanding is not her style. Those were her rookie years. She is over the glamorization of being a stripper, and her lack of social media accounts is a telltale sign. Meaning that making the guest list at the hottest nightclub is no longer a priority. There are no delusions of leaving the jungle at 35 to turn into a video vixen or landing the cover of a magazine flaunting her photoshopped cakes.

Whether she has a side job or stripping is a full-time gig, she knows her role in the jungle. She is aware of the other predators and their advantages over her. Having fake tits and a fake ass is not enough to compete. Managers hire newbies monthly, and amateur night is just an unpleasant reminder that predators are gunning for her spot on the roll call. No one feels the pressure of competition like the MILF. As a result, she aims to please.

While most young predators avoid being touchy-feely, the MILF takes full advantage of their reluctance to break the barrier of touch. Don't be surprised if she's sitting on your lap, slightly caressing your hand or giving you a snuggly hug. She uses touch to weaken your defenses, and that's a good thing. She's been around the block and giving high mileage lap dances is a badge of honor. A stroke of the ego here and a tug of your pride there (feel free to use your imagination) and you are in the presence of a professional who knows the game.

The MILF strategically focuses on a few targets using her energy wisely; she only eats what she kills. She knows that it's the quality of the customer, not the quantity. Too much rejection can trigger bitterness, so the smart MILFs maintain their poise and study their prey. In the jungle, the MILF is the crowned eagle that's always observing and patiently waiting. Suddenly, she'll swoop in and be right behind you, slowly easing into a quick neck massage; a skill that has become all but lost in jungles these days, hence the new trend of massage girls. Her touch instantly hits that spot that's been nagging at you all week. In a matter of seconds, you're on a resort island, feeling like a king, relaxed, and comfortable.

She whispers into your ear, "Hey sexy, what's your name?" "Well… you get settled in, and I'll be around."

Then she walks off sashaying with every curve in unison, proudly displaying all her tiger stripes for the jungle to see. Her confidence is dripping like sweat off her back as she gives you a quick glance and a look away, enough to start a seductive game of cat and mouse. Only someone with her experience is bold enough to *play* that game, but she's a veteran and knows that patience is one of her strengths. She can detect boredom like no other predator. Time will go by, and as soon as you think about making an early escape, that's when you'll feel those hands once again massaging your neck. Reminding you why you planned your trip and that a good time is only a green mile away. A MILF knows your intentions all too well, and she is more than ready to cater to your needs.

While your eyes fixate on the eye candy, always remember that experience and customer appreciation is a major part of the game. If you want the most "bang for your buck," you can always find the right MILF in the jungle that's willing to break a sweat and relieve your stress.

SURVIVOR NOTE

The 9's and 10's look good, but if you're going to get an Air Dance and terrible conversation, what's the point? Never settle for mediocre customer service. Be smart and embrace what the MILF has to offer.

LAW

13

ENJOY YOUR FAVORITE, BUT
DO NOT COMMIT TO
ONE STRIPPER

The relationship between a Regular and a
Favorite is a match made in strip club heaven. Only
those who have found that one magical, exotic
creature can testify to the power of this relationship.
It's the perfect union. It provides the necessary
balance that supports the entire strip club
ecosystem. The club gets their money to keep the
lights on, both parties (Regular and Favorite) get
what they want, and every level of the hierarchy of
needs is endorsed to the highest degree.

In your mind, you can have many Favorites.
Certainly, your imagination is allowed to run wild,

and when it comes to predators; the more, the merrier. The sheer number of g-strings that will catch your eye is endless. It's reminiscent to when Charles Darwin was observing species on his historic visit to Galapagos Islands. The overall impact can inspire a strip club version of the book *On the Origin of Species*. Several stage names will roll off your tongue with ease as you mentally conjure up a list of favorites: Bunnie, Ruby, Mellony, Ayana, Gianni, Mimi, Billie, Spice, Nadia, Katrina, Apple, Gucci, Alice, Persia, Bianca, and so on. However, once inside the jungle, where time and money are limited resources, only one name can carry the title of Favorite. Rightfully so, you know her schedule, and she is the sole reason you hit the ATM and planned a trip to the jungle.

A true Favorite knows exactly what buttons to push, and she's naturally in tune with your sexual side. There's very little role-play involved. There is no script to be read. Everything flows naturally. Where in most instances you have to re-enforce the notion that if she takes care of you, you'll take care of her; this goes without being said. You don't have to read between the lies. Mentally, you're both on the same wavelength. You speak the same erotic language. The conversation is flirty and playful, but yet still constructive and genuine; you may offer her great advice while she may give you moral support or vice versa. You two share secrets and personal information. She gives you what is called a GFE

(Girlfriend Experience)—without the stress and drama. There's even a solid chance of meeting outside the club, and into the concrete jungle.

Contrary to popular belief, the attraction is mutual. Albeit, the attraction can be on multiple levels. However, understand that money isn't the only factor that drives this relationship. There is a deep-rooted connection that for most is mysterious and unexplainable. It can be a plethora of things that captivate you; her eyes, curves, smile, voice, smell, walk, confidence, personality, or a tattoo inked in the right place. Maybe she mirrors a girl that you always wanted to date, or she's the polar opposite of the woman you're currently dating. Whatever the reason, the experience is almost mythical; like seeing a black panther up close in the wild. In your eyes, she's flawless, simply mesmerizing, and possesses the ability to have you forget about the dangers of the jungle all-together.

All in all, it's no surprise that she will receive the majority of your time and money, and you don't mind letting all the other predators know that she is the goddess of the jungle. But it's already quite evident, they can see the look in your eyes when you stare her up and down—it's clearly all about her!

But before you crown her your ATF (All-Time Favorite), it is also important that you subtly remind her from time to time that she is replaceable. Consider it a playful show of strip club gamesmanship between you and your Favorite. Do not waver from this reality. It is mandatory that you stick to your guns and establish an aura of authority. No matter your budget, you have leverage, and you must take advantage of your options.

There is no such thing as a commitment in the jungle.

Only Sugar Daddies and Whales have the resources to violate this natural law of the jungle. On every visit, they can cage a predator and prevent her from roaming around.

But the average patron has to understand that you can't wait on a stripper hand and foot. You are not a monogamous boyfriend waiting for your girlfriend while she shops at the mall. The capitalistic nature of the jungle dictates that you do not commit to one stripper. Comparatively, she will never fully commit to you. You can only tame a wild animal for so long, before their instincts to hunt and roam take over. So, while she's occupied, it is only right that you stay active and take care of your needs. You don't have to ask her for permission to survey the land. You are a survivor with standards and not a human ATM. Always keep a small discretionary fund for new encounters. However, while you explore your options, make sure that you select the right stripper for engagement. Your Favorite will be observing you out of the corner of her eye, wondering if you have good taste. For her, she's on the pursuit for defenseless prey. It's all about a quick kill and stuffing her bag full of money, before ultimately returning to you and reassuring your Regular status. But for you, while you roam the jungle, she will be evaluating your appetite; deciding if you're still worthy of special treatment.

Choose a stripper that she secretly can't stand, and you will undoubtedly lose major points. But if she approves of your selection, then your value as a Regular will increase. You will also create a competitive edge. Strippers are not immune to bouts of jealousy, especially if they feel that they have a solid grasp on a Regular who showers them with money and adoration. They are territorial when it comes to their customer base. Once you walk into the jungle, your Favorite can already estimate a dollar amount that you will spend. Immediately, she starts calculating her bills and future purchases. But once you venture off and find an equally exotic predator, she will be alarmed and instantly reminded that your company is valuable, and of course, your money. Losing your business is a blow to her ego and bank account—never forget that!

By choosing to spend your money on the competition, her animal instincts to be defensive heighten. In her eyes, you are a Regular who aims for the best service and she won't hesitate to oblige to your standards. Remember, apex predators respect other apex predators. They have strong egos and superficial reputations within the ecosystem.

They enjoy the bragging rights of having a loyal and generous client; one who has a preference for identifying the best stripper in the club.

However, if she doesn't appreciate you and your steady business, do not hesitate to find a new Favorite. This is the reason why aficionados use the term CF (Current Favorite). It's a subtle reminder to oneself that *currently*—anyone can be replaced. A stripper should always treat her clientele with a high level of respect. As soon as she takes you for granted, keep it moving and don't look back. Although you may be dismayed by her sudden act of neglect, stay focused and realize that it's the predatory nature of the jungle. Everyone is trying to survive.

At the same time, your Favorite has the option to choose a new Regular at any moment; money talks and you're not the only one who can fall for a big butt and a smile. Even if you've built a steamy relationship based on flirtatiousness, secrecy, and erotic reciprocity, that doesn't guarantee you a say-so in her decision to choose up. It's her job to chase the money, devour prey, and leave the remains for the Vultures.

SURVIVOR NOTE

Enjoy your Favorite, savor the cozy time spent together in VIP, but do not commit to her fully; embracing the fact that you have options is key to your survival. And surviving the jungle is the only commitment that should be made.

LAW
14

PERFECT THE DRIZZLE

MAKE IT RAIN

Ever since Fat Joe and Lil Wayne delivered
the strip club anthem, "Make it Rain" in 2006, the
industry has been dealing with a paradigm shift in
tipping behavior. For a multitude of impressionable
patrons, tipping was redefined, but unfortunately, it
took on a narcissistic point of view. With its catchy
chorus and instructive video on how to rapidly peel
off dollar bills, the song struck the strip club
industry like an earthquake. The impact created a
tsunami of influence that engulfed strippers,
patrons, and even outsiders. Making it rain became
a part of popular culture; a new catchphrase was
added to the strip club lexicon, and strippers

celebrated as the sales of umbrellas went through the roof. This paradigm shift brought in a flashy attitude towards tipping that mimicked the gaudy and grandiose lifestyles endorsed by rappers. On the one hand, business increased, and the rain never stopped, and on the other hand, egotism spread throughout the jungles like a plague.

In today's strip club climate, making it rain has now become more about the tipper and not the target. Although survivors respect the impact of Fat Joe, Lil Wayne, and a host of other rappers who have promoted the art of rainmaking, a lawful patron does not take his cues from rappers. They are predominantly concerned with holding a crown and being the center of attention, even if it's in a room full of sexy strippers. Those self-centered, lawless values are necessary for survival in the world of hip hop, but they have no place in the jungle. Many have adopted a mentality that is rooted in narcissism to the point where their primary goal is to compete for attention reserved for strippers; they want all eyes on them. Acting as if they are a celebrity "hosting" a special event. Never mind the g-stringed predators roaming around, the focus is on the patron who's making it rain with his self-centered agenda. That mentality has more to do about the desperate need for attention than maximizing one's five senses during a lap dance.

On the surface, making it rain may seem like harmless fun. In a capitalistic environment where he who has the cash rules; spreading the wealth with generosity is considered kinglike. Thinking economically and valuing every cent is seen as unkinglike. That's why some patrons are so self-absorbed with making it rain. It gives them the false sense of being the King of the Jungle.

But there is no king. There is no crown. There is only survival.

The dirty secret is that most patrons make it rain to impress other patrons. They can care less about investing and fostering a relationship with a potential Favorite or pursuing the sacred lap dance. Many are willing to blow money just to play the temporary role of "the star" in their imaginary rap video, and lo and behold, you and the strippers are the extras. They are celebrity-driven, and can't wait to leave the club and post their absurd levels of showmanship on social media.

This no-holds-barred-stance on making it rain may rub some the wrong way. Mention this law and you can see the reaction of those guilty of creating torrential rains with the purpose of vanity. Some strippers will read this law and quickly give a side-eye. Automatically assuming that savvy patrons are trying to knock their hustle, but that's far from the case. As stated in Law 6, Always Tip With Purpose; a non-tipper in a club is the epitome of tackiness. So, one may ask, "is it ever appropriate to make it rain?"

Of course, as long as you are strategic with your rainmaking. Whether you are enjoying a stage dance or a table dance, it's best to produce rain as an element of surprise; something to be appreciated, like finally receiving raindrops in a severe drought. At its very foundation, rainmaking is simply an extravagant way of tipping. Special events, birthdays, and celebrations are all occasions that can use some downpour—think of it as strip club party confetti.

But the real issue is about being economical. If the law is to always tip with purpose, then the rule is to only make it rain with an agenda. If a stripper has to hide from your rainfall, ensure that she ends up running for shelter in a lap dance booth or VIP room. If it's your Favorite's birthday, that is the ideal time to shower her with tips, letting her know that you appreciate all the extracurricular activity. Watch her eyes light up as she receives the green carpet treatment. If you want to make a lasting impression, grab a money gun and take aim at the ceiling. She will feel honored to witness your 21-money gun salute. However, unless you're a Whale with deep pockets, and you work for a scholarship fund, don't get caught up in the hype of establishing a reputation as a rainmaker; the self-proclaimed King of the Jungle. In a cruel way, strippers will expect you to maintain that reputation on every visit. Once you can't provide the spectacle, they will turn to the next patron who's peeling away. You will be a victim of your own creation.

MAKE IT DRIZZLE

Instead of making it rain and showering an entire stage full of strippers, it is far more effective to select a primary target and drizzle her with tips. This action is appropriately called "Making it Drizzle." It's the Warren Buffett approach to tipping as opposed to the flashiness promoted by rappers. It is best to keep things low-key and unassuming. Let your money talk, but never give a hint of how much you're holding. Take one look at Warren Buffett. Does he look like one of the richest men in the world?

Therein lies one of the benefits of making it drizzle. You can create intrigue and an air of mystery. She will never know if you're making your money stretch or if you're working with a secret stash. And if you perfect the drizzle, she will stick around to find out. You set the pace and as long as you keep tipping in increments, you can observe and gauge her level of hustle—carefully watching her every move and facial expression. Just like a watering can, let the light rain trickle down, dollar by dollar. This concept is the real meaning of "trickle-down economics." Unlike the highly debatable theory first introduced as a political zinger, this economic idea is proven to be efficient and beneficial to both parties inside the jungle.

If any stripper disagrees with this sentiment, just ask her this question. Would you rather divide $100 in singles between a wild pack of Piranhas or receive the total $100 in a one-on-one, trickle-down session? In that instant, you will see the fascination with rain lose out to the bare necessities. If she wants to be a team player and divide, then fine, just increase the dollar amount to $200 and watch how she starts to respect the drizzle.

With every fine drop, you are creating momentum. If your plan is to get a lap dance, you can make it drizzle to get her attention, read between the lies, and then leave a trail of sprinkles leading to a booth. Or, if you're on a tight budget, you can focus on a target, drizzle her with tips, and then set up a one-on-one session for your next trip. Ultimately, you are using your dollars to build stripper equity. Your time and money are an investment and part of your agenda is to get a return on that investment. Considering the financial risk of blowing a bunch of money by throwing it in the air, making it drizzle is the best way to let your interest mature over time.

Akin to elephants, strippers have amazing memories and they never forget a patron who tips on a consistent basis. Stability in the jungle is hard to come by, and the reputation of a drizzler is highly respected; it just lacks popularity. But popularity is not the goal. Only a rookie believes that there are legitimate bragging rights in creating a spectacle for all to see. It doesn't take much thought and effort to toss a wad of cash at a stripper and look around for applause. Anyone can make it rain. The spotlight is already on you, so there is no need to battle predators for center stage to see who can provide the best show.

Ask yourself this question, "What is the difference between a drizzler that has $300 and a rainmaker that has $300? Strategy. At the end of the trip, one will survive, and the other will suffer a self-inflicted internal wound to the ego.

It is best to perfect the drizzle and be economical.

SURVIVOR NOTE

Instead of making it rain with charitable intent, concentrate your resources on one target and drizzle her with tips, dollar by dollar. Tipping is an investment and perfecting the drizzle is the economical way to build stripper equity and minimize the risk of blowing your budget.

LAW
15

THE ONLY RELATIONSHIP THAT MATTERS IS THE ONE INSIDE THE JUNGLE

From the onset, the intention of this book was to strip away the facade and glamorization of the gentlemen's club. One topic that deserves an honest discourse is the lofty pursuit of dating a stripper—not finding a Favorite—but turning a GFE (Girlfriend Experience) into a real GF (Girlfriend). The ever-enticing challenge to walk into the jungle and not only survive, but to tranquilize, capture, and ultimately domesticate a wild animal. Some veterans brag about their big-game hunting skills and proudly show off their conquest like taxidermy trophies to separate the men from the boys.

It is understandable that once you get a whiff of a stripper's sex appeal, it's practically impossible not to fantasize about a one-night stand or a lustful getaway. It's not shocking when an older patron receives a mind-blowing lap dance and quickly submits his application for Sugar Daddy status—sponsoring trips and showering her with gifts. Any veteran can empathize when a young patron catches feelings and falls victim to his patriarchal instinct to be a knight in shining armor. He foolishly takes on the self-appointed mission of rescuing her from the trappings and tawdriness of the strip club life, even though leaving "the life" is the last thing on her mind. Any patron can fathom being in the presence of a sexy waitress and resisting the temptation to ask her out. You're intrigued by the fact that she works in such a sexual environment, and you can't help but wonder if she has hidden twerk skills.

Every scenario you can think of comes as no surprise. The thrill of taking things outside the jungle opens up a whole new world of possibility and that's why for most patrons, dating a stripper is a legitimate goal. However, this book is not about selling you a fantasy, that's the stripper's job. You can google and find tons of blogs, YouTube tutorials, and books on how to date a stripper. There are strip club shysters that host seminars teaching patrons the proven techniques of bagging a Tiger, even though they can't show you any evidence of their track record; good luck on getting a refund for that purchase. Apparently, one rule of thumb is never to pay for a lap dance because if you do, she will forever see you as a customer, but ensure that you're a generous tipper. Really? Not only is that a blatant violation to the hierarchy of needs, but also when does a survivor take his cues from strip club charlatans? Get this straight, as soon as you walk into the jungle, you are a customer; there's no ifs, ands, or buts about it. It just depends on what type of customer you are. Running from that truth and making decisions based on perception is pointless. That mentality will render you powerless. Any rule or law dealing with a gentlemen's club should empower you. By all means, go ahead and have fun, get a lap dance, and be a *customer*—just be a smart one.

Indeed, it's possible to make a romantic connection with a stripper, they are human after all. This is a reference to actually getting acquainted beyond exchanging phone numbers and being told the sacred government name. Just like most girls, they like to cuddle, watch Netflix and chill, and get wined and dined. And there are pros to dating a stripper. Since you've already seen her birthday suit, you can bypass the topic of sexuality and deal with the inner person. There's no perceived hidden agenda. She looks good naked; now you can proceed to the next question. However, to reach that point, there is a considerable amount of time and effort spent inside and outside the jungle to make a genuine connection. You will have to prove yourself a worthy candidate and one who is not addicted to the jungle. With all that investment and wishful thinking, there's still no guarantee that you'll even get close to a spooning session. You are, in essence, investing in a *pipe* dream. When it comes to the jungle, there is a secret adage that must be learned:

A booty in your hand is worth more than dating to get the bush.

The cardinal rule is to spend your time and money wisely and when you're in the jungle getting a lap dance, holding a hand full of booty, why concern yourself with anything outside the jungle? Your five senses are busy at work and you're getting the most out of your dollars. The only relationship that should matter is the one right there inside. Maximizing your time in the jungle is the better return on your investment. Always focus on "the moment" and taking care of your needs while on the clock. If you stick to your guns and adhere to this law, everything else, like a natural pair of boobs will fall into place. You'll be surprised at the phone numbers that come your way when *dating* is the last thing on your mind. Your carefree energy will attract the friskiest predators. If she wants more than a customer relationship; a one-night stand, dinner date, or a friend with benefits, she will let you know—it's that simple.

Don't even entertain the thought of dating a stripper because you have no idea what's in store. Can you honestly handle a predator who has no plans on leaving the jungle? As the saying goes, *be careful what you wish for.* One doesn't have to demonize strippers to point out the potential headaches that you may encounter. You don't need to delve into a stripper's psyche and learn her family history to predict a level of drama coming your way. That's unnecessary; no one is trying to disrespect the hustle and look down on those who work the pole because at the end of the day—strippers need love too. And many will surprise you. Behind their sexual personas are down-to-earth chicks that can teach you a lot about life.

But this law is rooted in practicality. The goal is to stay grounded and deal with the obvious. You're dealing with women with hectic schedules; some sleep during the day and work all night or vice versa. Have you ever dealt with a woman that doesn't work a 9 to 5? These women are used to fast cash, and they're not accustomed to waiting two weeks for a payday. Routing numbers and direct-deposits are old-school concepts, they're too busy counting cash at the end of the night like human money machines. Whether they know it or not, their life is trapped in the fast lane.

So, while you're stuck at your messy cubicle

loading a stapler and trying to figure out how many vacation days you have left, she's on social media posting a picture of her arrival at Miami International Airport. Next week she's picking up her tickets at "will call" for the Lakers versus Clippers game, courtesy of a 6'7 bench warmer. There's also those backstage passes given by the latest R&B sensation with a six-pack and neck tattoos.

Even if you're not trying to catch up with an aspiring socialite who's going 100 mph, the average low-key stripper is still buying bottles and partying up a storm with her female-only entourage.

If that doesn't open your eyes, you may encounter a different type of stripper—the one who continually flakes on you because she's struggling to balance mommy duties while splitting custody with her baby daddy. You're thinking about off the wall sex, and she's thinking reruns of 90's sitcoms. She is only sexual in the jungle. In fact, the stage is her primary source of excitement. When you see her twerking, the last thing on your mind is finding out that she's an undercover couch potato who's addicted to wearing sweatpants.

It is also impossible to forget about the stripper who has the ex-boyfriend who can't stay out of the picture. You're trying to enjoy a coffee date, but you keep noticing a muscle head guy covered in tattoo sleeves eyeing you from afar. Are you ready to watch your back from ex-boyfriends that attach themselves like a ball and chain? The smart answer is no.

Once you consider the typical lifestyle of a stripper, the pursuit of dating one doesn't sound so appealing. Don't let the fantasy of a sexual conquest warp your reality. With a stripper, there is a strong probability of great sex, but either way, you'll never know what you're going to get. The smart patron has already contemplated all these dating scenarios and realizes that the best date is the one right there in VIP.

SURVIVOR NOTE

Keeping things within the boundaries of the jungle forces you to maximize your time and money inside. It also saves you precious resources and eliminates the potential drama that comes with investing in a pipe dream.

LAW
16

RESPECT THE HUSTLE

For many, it's difficult to deal with the
inconvenient truth that being a stripper is a job. It's
a legitimate hustle. They clock in, and they clock
out just like the rest of working class America.
Nothing says *hard* labor like giving a raincoater a
touchy lap dance. That sketchy part of the job takes
sacrifice and mental fortitude. But to the masses of
outsiders, this is unconventional wisdom. The
traditional view is that strippers occupy an isolated
stage away from society. Even though strip clubs are
becoming more mainstream and some ex-strippers
are enjoying a pseudo-celebrity status, no stripper
would dare put their seductive skills on a one-page
resume. A stripper is not a member of the
underground economy, but her occupation still

doesn't fit the definition of what many consider a "good" job. Don't be fooled by the superficial love given by desperate housewives who take pole dance classes. They have absolutely no allegiance to g-stringed predators. They may fantasize about having the sex appeal of a Tiger, and playfully discuss the importance of knowing how to twerk, but they will never be in favor of a job that can wreck their household in one measly song.

In reality, when push comes to shove, many in the mainstream are unable to conceal their preconceived notions, labels, assumptions, and stigmas about strippers. But it doesn't matter where this flashy profession ranks within the hierarchy of adult entertainment— it's a job. Strippers are hustlers in the truest sense. They're independent contractors with no HR manager (sorry House Mom) to explain to them the details of their 401k plans or healthcare packages. In fact, there's no stripper retirement plan, no pension, no union, and no safety net—just a pair of fishnets!

They can only rely on the hustle. A hustle that is dependent on self-motivation and self-confidence with the hopes of earning enough money to be self-sufficient. If you think it's tough for the average person to stand on their own two feet, just imagine twerking for hours in 6 1/2 inch stilettos. Given that strippers physically and mentally meet these challenges head on, it's only right to acknowledge the amount of hustle that they possess.

Part-Time Therapist. There is a lot that you can learn from these inhabitants of the jungle. Not only are they experts on male sexuality, knowing first-hand that men are visual creatures that can't survive on visuals alone, they know that patrons need therapy sessions to release stress and escape reality. They're keenly aware of the internal battle that many face between being a saint and a sinner. That's why they always have an open seat available on their favorite couch. And truth be told, they can relate because they also struggle with the same internal battle. Society labels them the sinner, but behind the confessional booth, they are a saint for so many, and patrons can certainly testify to their devoutness to their profession.

These consultations are healthy and stress relieving. But academia will never give enough credit to these part-time therapists. Those in the mental health community will point to their lack of credentials and licenses, but patrons will just point to the soreness in their neck. When it comes to getting stuff off your chest, patrons will always prefer the open ear of a stripper, especially if she's hands on. Even though at the end of the session, one is diagnosed with blue balls and Post Traumatic Sprung Disorder (PTSD). But as long as you escape the jungle with a temporary smile, one is more than happy to make a return visit.

Business-Minded. Strippers are also masters at straddling the thin line between business and pleasure. A balancing act that is harder than any pole trick they can try to pull off. Similar to a successful CEO, their job is to focus on the bottom line, and that's making a profit and taking care of their shareholders (bills, family, and friends). Those in tune with the hustle know there is money to be made and fun to be had. But first, there is money to be made. A stripper can be in full twerk mode, smiling up a storm, giving you a wink of an eye, but mentally she's thinking about the numbers on her balance sheet. She has a particular bill that needs to be paid off and she won't let pleasure distract her from the business at hand. Once again, being a stripper is a job—a job that requires maturity.

There's certainly no time to waste on water-cooler talk. The smart ones know that gossip and drama are bad for business. They not only respect the code of silence, they understand it's a necessity. Privacy is to be cherished. Although you do have a few reckless strippers that believe they are legitimate celebrities and they can't wait for thirsty publishers and television producers to promote their tell-all lifestyles, the majority of strippers are business-minded women who only want to stack money, have fun, and go home after their shift.

Survival of the Fittest. Regardless of the personal reasons that lead them to the stripper pole, you must respect the go-getter mentality of those that are willing to survive the jungle. The jungle is not for the weak-minded and fragile. A lot of girls find out the hard way. They see one stripper flashing a brick of cash on social media, and they automatically think it's easy money. These girls are given the false impression that every patron is a human ATM just waiting to spit out cash for the slightest glance of a bikini bottom. But nothing comes easy in the jungle. There are no cakewalks. Even the best in the business have slow days. The dreams of heavy rain can quickly turn into nightmares of mercy tips. All of a sudden, twerking for 8 hours doesn't seem so fun when your calf muscles are tightening up and corns start popping up out of nowhere.

It's easy to see the cash, but many can't imagine the drama that comes with the territory— the catfights, the rampant jealousy, the flaky relationships, and brutal competition. Only the strong survive. Keep in mind, there is no Stripper Hall of Fame where one can hang up their stilettos and showcase their game worn g-strings. When a veteran retires, only a handful of Regulars are there to applaud her exit. She will leave the game quietly, mostly with regrets and a bag full of memories. Most patrons wouldn't even notice her absence, and the ones that do have already found her replacement.

When a stripper gains weight, ages, or loses her top-notch status, her co-workers secretly relish, taking advantage and seizing the opportunity to flaunt their toned bodies in front of her trusted clients. Strippers are cannibalistic, and in the game —the ends justify the means.

There is no mercy in the jungle. The jungle doesn't care about feelings and personal issues. So, when you encounter a stripper that is about her business, clear the way and respect the hustle. She is surviving in an environment that won't blink twice when she stumbles and falls. All eyes are on her, and being objectified at every step can take a toll on one mentally, yet they still survive the harshness of the jungle. The last thing they need is a patron with an unhealthy attitude. The type of visitor that not only fails to check his jealousy at the door, but his baggage as well—anger towards women, bitterness, and blatant disrespect. The atmosphere doesn't need that type of energy, and regardless of what you think about strippers, they don't deserve your bad vibes. It's their territory, and you have no license to walk into their place of work with your moral judgments. Would you like someone to go to your job and shame your every move? Exactly.

Diversity. Respect the fact that every stripper brings something different to the table. They all have their niche within the stripper ecosystem. Just because a particular stripper is not your cup of tea, doesn't mean she doesn't play a vital role in creating the strip club experience. Never knock the hustle of those trying to survive the best way they know how. Diversity is what makes the jungle full of possibility and surprise. The Tiger, the MILF, the grumpy and bitter, the Piranha, the Vulture, even the Professional Air Dancer all have a right to coexist in the jungle. And that's just a handful of strippers fighting for territory. It's normal to have a preference and a craving for a specific look or skill, but it's important to appreciate the overall range of styles. You can't have a stripper food chain without multiple levels of predators. Not every stripper is a certified booty shaker. When it comes to working the pole, not every stripper is a Romanian gymnast. Some strippers don't have enough ass to be a twerk champion, and many lack the athletic ability to compete in stripper pole gymnastics—and that's okay.

Some strippers have to rely more on a flirty conversation than making it clap. Others lean on their non-verbal skills. They specialize in giving eye contact that makes you feel compelled to engage. Whatever the tactic, those that can't demand the spotlight have to find a way *to get in where they fit in.*

This is why most strippers focus so much on presentation. Just like in the animal kingdom, natural selection has created some eye-catching coloration that makes the average person look twice.

Inside the jungle, this array of diversity is no different. There are those with funky hairstyles; braids, buzz cuts, pigtails, rainbow hues, and dip-dyes. Then, there is the creative world of stripper (stiletto) nails. Some resembling tiger claws and shark teeth. These works of art are hard to miss, and once they put their grapplers in you—surrender and hand over your cash.

Everyone is already familiar with the power of tattoos and their ability to make any hustler standout from the pack. Strippers alone keep the tattoo industry hard at work. Along the same lines, strippers also know about the magnetic attraction that happens when they show a pair of nipple piercings.

You'll also see colorful bodysuits, fishnets, leggings, rompers, teddies, and micro skirts. As far as stripper shoes, there's platforms, stilettos, ankle boots, knee high sandals, and flashy heels covered in fringe—anything to accentuate their unique qualities.

With the normalcy of plastic surgery and ass shots, always respect a stripper who wants to proudly display her natural body. Do not lose perspective on the beauty of a body that was God-given vs. man-made. A body that has not gone under the knife and avoided a needle is rare and unique. Sadly, being all-natural is an old-school hustle.

Top of the Food Chain. To respect the hustle is also to respect their high-ranking position within the strip club ecosystem. Strippers are the apex predators, the ones brave enough to work the pole, risking their sanity and personal reputation. During a dancer roll call, they stand exposed, placed on display for every patron to see. And they are the only ones who walk into the darkness of a VIP room and return victorious, leaving a trail of wounded prey.

Never confuse their dominant position with that of a waitress or a bartender who wants to twerk on the side and grab attention away from the stage. Do not give the slightest impression that you put them on the same level. Until they make that bold decision to "flash for cash", they are secondary and primary predators. Always respect the natural order in the jungle. Everyone knows that if you eliminate strippers, the entire strip club industry crumbles. You'll just be surviving at a typical dive bar. So, tip your waitress and bartender, but make sure you provide the majority of your resources for the ultimate hustler—the stripper.

SURVIVOR NOTE

To match wits and gamesmanship with a stripper, you must have a healthy outlook on the jungle and a high-level of respect for the hustle. This respect will allow you to see eye to eye with a stripper, and in return, she will respect you. Understand that you both need each other to survive and keep the industry alive.

LAW
17

MASTER THE ART OF TIMING: DAY-SHIFT VS. NIGHT-SHIFT

Timing is of the essence, and the decision of when to enter the jungle and how long you *plan* to stay is critical to your survival. The key word is "plan." Because once you get caught in the clutches of a predator, it is not uncommon to lose track of time. There is no greater example of being a prisoner of the moment than being mesmerized during a high mileage lap dance. A quick stop can easily turn into a 5-hour rendezvous.

For the vast majority of patrons, time and money are limited resources. It may be exciting to fantasize about making it rain for 40 days and 40 nights, but this book is not about reciting strip club parables. If you need empirical evidence, just try pussyfooting around the wrong stripper with mindless chatter and empty pockets; she'll tell you point blank that *time is money.*

The quickest way to be chewed and spat out is to waste those resources aimlessly. You don't visit the jungle for a pat on the back or to receive a participation trophy. Furthermore, you don't spend money in hopes of receiving a free pass for your next visit. You're on the clock, and businesslike is the desired approach.

Given that a predator will strike at any moment, you must understand the environment and the time of day in which they strike. There is a significant difference between a nocturnal stripper and a diurnal stripper. The latter is not a familiar term, but there's no coincidence why Sugar Daddies make their rounds during the day and those looking for a party atmosphere make their appearances at night.

Once you identify and comprehend the differences, then you can begin to exercise mastery over the inner working of the Day-Shift versus the Night-Shift. Each shift provides unique challenges and contrasting predatory behaviors. The seasoned patron can adapt and manipulate a given environment to their advantage and maintain focus on their primary goal.

DAY-SHIFT

According to outsiders, there is still a stigma about walking into a jungle while the sun is out. Many say that the freaks come out at night, but the raincoaters creep during the day.

One must ask yourself, "When was the last time an outsider bought you a lap dance?"

Only rookies have the audacity to *sleep* on the Day-Shift—specifically, the early afternoon until eight o'clock. Seasoned survivors know all about the benefits of making daylight excursions. It's not just to avoid a cover charge or take advantage of Happy Hour prices. Those are perks, but the real benefits are subtle and situational.

Nocturnal strippers are not the only ones who like to have fun. Diurnal strippers are equally as fun-filled and ready to blow off some steam. They may be juggling a job, attending night school, or just occupied with other priorities that won't allow them to work during the party hours. As a result, you are dealing with professionals who are skilled and adept at customer relations. They don't have the luxury of dealing with multiple targets—less patrons means a smaller margin for error. They come to work focused and eager to play, and it's up to you to take advantage.

For the average nocturnal stripper with ADD (Attention Deficit Disorder), the Day-Shift is frightening. Inactivity during the day is more severe and detrimental to a stripper's psyche. Their worst fear is spending more money on gas than the amount they make at the jungle. Not having enough money for tip out is a big blow to their ego, so it's only instinctual for those who choose to work during the day to be on the hustle—go big or go home. They can't rely on a party atmosphere for their enjoyment. They have to be able to hunt alone and be successful at all costs.

Diurnal strippers are more likely to encourage conversation and push for a lap dance— bravo! They're naturally suited for the one-on-one battle. They dread hearing a stage call from the DJ signaling that they have to perform for the few in attendance and mercy tips are not encouraging. However, that's a good thing. Their stage performance is more of conduit for a lap dance or a VIP—check their faces. They can't wait for the second song to end. They'd rather be in a dark corner with you discussing the hierarchy of needs. You will be amazed at how easy it is to read between the lies when they're faced with extreme boredom and stagnation.

Unlike the Night-Shift, the Day-Shift has fewer patrons which makes it easy to avoid troublemakers and lawless spectators. This benefit is what Sugar Daddies have long mastered. Their time is precious, and they don't waste it weaving through civilians, bumping into rookies, and entertaining frivolous pursuits. They enjoy a peaceful setting, a cocktail, and the pleasure of avoiding the flashiness and tackiness of the uninformed. Do yourself a favor and learn from Sugar Daddies. A relaxed atmosphere is perfect for you to concentrate on your agenda and maximize your resources.

On top of that, the security is more likely to look the other way. From their standpoint, who wants to get into a disagreement with a patron around two o'clock in the day? They figure that you're spending good money, so why interfere? They just want their shift to end.

The DJ is also less likely to single you out for having unlawful strip club etiquette. Being shamed by the DJ for not tipping or displaying inappropriate behavior is never a good look. It's the DJ's job to instigate and promote activity within the ecosystem, but during the day, they understand the need to give patrons less of a hassle.

Smart patrons not only take advantage of the intimacy and the low-key atmosphere of the day, but once you have a good rapport with your Favorite, you can always request her to switch up her schedule and take a three o'clock meeting with you and your main couch. It's like catching a predator and transporting her to a new, isolated zoo. Instead of juggling patrons and bouncing around, she can now give you all the attention in the world.

NIGHT-SHIFT

The positives of the Night-Shift are so widely known and embraced that the negatives are never discussed; they're just quietly tolerated. It's easy to ignore the pitfalls when the nightlife keeps you distracted and nervously on the edge of your seat.

The average person in society is socially conditioned to enjoy the darkness of the night, and when entering the mistiness of a dimly lit strip club, the transition is seamless—it's second nature.

As soon as the clock strikes eight, the jungle starts to come alive. The DJ begins to deliver his comical one-liners, echoing those familiar 2 for 1 specials, and the clarion roll call of strippers. The security puff out their chests more, letting the crowd know that tonight is not the night for mischief. The waitresses make their rounds while serving up sexy smiles. The "massage girl" warms up, stretching her fingers, preparing for a long night. And at the top of the food chain, the apex predators, and the money-hungry creep into the landscape. The snakes slither around corners, the Piranhas start to unite, and the felines slow down to a cat-like creep.

The stripper ecosystem is full of life and abundance. The number of strippers alone is worth the cover; all types of predators in one room looking for prey. More predators, brings more patrons, and with more patrons, brings more money—and that brings, even more, predators. Therefore, the Night-Shift business cycle revolves, intertwined and camouflaged in a party atmosphere.

Your adrenaline reaches a boiling point, as your eyes scan the jungle for danger. But not all party favors provide the right inspiration.

There's no doubt that the Night-Shift is for the survivors. If you find a Tiger, you better hold on to its tail. You're not the only one looking to get a lap dance from exotic animals. The added competition can make one feel uneasy, especially when it comes to your Favorite. You must check your jealousy at the door and have a plan for survival because she will be pulled in many directions by thirsty patrons. In one instant; she can disappear in the blink of an eye. Sugar Daddies creep during the Day-Shift, but at night, a Whale can show up and tie up your Favorite for hours with no apologies. You'll simply have to deal with it.

On the Night-Shift, predators also feel the intense competition. Some turn it up a notch and bring out their secret weapons. Others fall into the background and lose confidence in their hustle.

A good number of predators, who should be on their A-game, take an easy route when getting their money. They passively transform into stage dancers, camouflaging themselves into the crowded stage and hiding out for hours. They're content with their little space and collection of light rain. As long as the party atmosphere continues, they're okay with settling for tips and not giving lap dances.

Unlike the Day-Shift, real estate and elbow room are scarce. You must stake out your territory, whether with a cushy seat, a VIP table or better yet, a VIP couch. If you want to make a big impression, you can always have fun in the champagne room. Space is critical to one's ability to think clearly; congestion leads to irritation and anxiety.

Unfortunately, more patrons also mean more spectators. Not everyone comes to the jungle to survive. Too many patrons come for the jungle safari tour. They're in close quarters, sitting comfortably and safely in a cushioned seat, watching the wildlife with binoculars. They want to feel the rush and adrenaline of the hunt without actually roaming the jungle and getting their hands dirty. They imagine the thrills of receiving a lap dance but are afraid of earning the scars. They may tip a dollar every couple of hours and babysit the same drink they bought when they entered, but by no means do they want to "rumble in the jungle." Apex predators can sense a spectator's fear and absence of will. They leave these types of patrons for the Vultures of the jungle that feed from dead conversation and scraps off the main floor.

SURVIVOR NOTE

Exercising mastery over the inner working of the Day-Shift versus the Night-Shift is the mark of a true survivor. Both shifts provide clear advantages and disadvantages that affect your agenda. Time and money are limited resources, and knowing the differences between the shifts and its population of predators is key to using your resources wisely.

LAW
18

FIND A MOLE (STRIPPER AGENT):
INFORMATION IS PRICELESS

As you frequent your favored jungle, several different relationships will develop over time. It is most likely that you will have a Favorite, a solid go-to waitress and an overall rapport with staff. Some of you may even have a DJ welcome you in with a head nod and a shout-out, signaling to the predators that a familiar face has arrived. If you've proven to be a patron that is knowledgeable of the laws, one who knows the ways of the jungle and survives, your business will be respected. A reputation as a Regular will resonate and spread throughout the land like wildfire. Exercise a high level of discretion and you'll be regarded as a gentleman. With a solid reputation, you can establish a relationship with one of the few assets in the jungle: the Mole.

Every loyal patron needs a trusted resource for inside information. The strip club industry is inherently cutthroat and constantly adapting to societal pressures and commercial issues that affect its bottom line. Every jungle is a reflection of the competitive environment and through all the unpredictable changes that happen in the industry, who do you think will be the one stuck in the dark, and left to fend for themselves? You. While your hands are full dealing with predators, it's far too easy to get blindsided by the nature of the business. Understand that any information that is detrimental to your agenda will be hard to come by. There's no weekly newsletter sent out that will notify you about the temperature changes in the jungle. That's why a Mole is a prized asset. Acquiring valuable intel can help you to stay ahead of the game, avoid traps, and prevent sneak attacks. According to managers and predators, business is always on the up-and-up, and there's always an ATM close by. In their eyes, competition doesn't exist. They have a vested interest in promoting their jungle as the best adventure in town. You can't blame them. It's all part of the game.

But you should know better. Jungles are bloodthirsty environments, and as a result, there is always a substantial amount of dirt and turmoil going on behind the scenes. Owners often clash with the local government; citations are frequently given, and strict rules are gladly broken. Also, new regulations are implemented without notice. A change in management can wipe out an entire stripper ecosystem and replace them with a completely new breed of air and stage dancers. Your favorite club for high mileage has undergone some changes, and guess who will be the last to know? You.

When it comes to strippers, it's never a surprise when you hear vicious rumors floating around about a jungle's demise or the scandalous reasons on why to avoid this jungle and that jungle. Although these rumors are usually started by disgruntled strippers who were fired or decided to join a rival club, there is often some atom of truth behind the slander. Also, every stripper knows the shady tricks that their co-workers play on naive patrons. Every night they rub shoulders with Shady Accountant Lap Dancers, scammers, and bloodsuckers. They have endless stories about catfights, cat burglars, and drama queens that love to spread gossip. But be very careful. Word on the street travels, and it's difficult to distinguish between gossip and truth. Gossip is a waste of time, and false information can put you at a disadvantage. You cannot establish a solid reputation by being a chatty patty. That's why receiving secret information from a reliable source is priceless. It saves you time and money.

Strip club aficionados try their best to gain

an advantage by creating underground websites and forums that provide intel. These destinations act as the intelligence agencies for brethren trying to prepare for the ever-evolving jungle. Another option is to finesse a relationship with a waitress, DJ, or bartender. They are the proverbial fly on the wall, and they always have relevant information to share. But without a doubt, the ideal Mole is a stripper— one who can mentally and physically hold her own. If you find her, you will be in the presence of the perfect spy, the hidden owl sitting on a branch in the midst of the jungle. She's the one with the front row seat, watching all the activity, and taking mental notes. When she gets money-hungry, she just swoops down and grabs her prey with her talons and then returns to stealth mode. And just like an owl, her keen sense of hearing comes in handy when she's sitting in the dressing room overhearing every gripe and concern. Given her status in the club, she is the first to receive updates from management and competition is constantly trying to get her to jump clubs. Naturally, it's her job to keep an ear out to the streets and her eyes on the money.

So if you hear a rumor that your favorite jungle temporarily lost its liquor license, you can quickly contact her for the 411. She'll give you the real scoop and possibly save you a trip. Plus, there's nothing worse than driving a long distance and discovering that your number one hangout is only serving overpriced bottled waters and energy drinks.

What if you hear rumbles that your treasured nude club just got raided by Vice? Who do you turn to? Is this a rumor created by competition? Your Mole can be hard at work getting you the tough answers. The last thing you want is to be in VIP getting interrupted by the boys in blue. Rumors like this will have patrons scared to enter the parking lot.

What if you received a disturbing phone call from a confidant telling you that there's a temporary no-touch rule on lap dances? Before you can shed a tear, your Mole has informed you the reason and the best time to return.

What if your Favorite is missing in action? You're starting to believe the rumors of an early retirement from the strip club game? Your Mole is right there to console you. She can inform you that your Favorite just went on sabbatical. And don't be surprised if she returns with some enhancements.

What about the new jungle that's opening up across town? It's supposed to be a celebrity hangout; a tropical rainforest with non-stop precipitation. There's rumors of a mass exodus of predators who want to pay lower tip out fees and work more flexible hours, and enjoy the cash flow of a new river. Your Mole can tell you who's thinking about leaving or staying.

These are just a few of the unforeseen challenges that a Mole can help you maneuver around. The benefits of having someone on the *inside* of the jungle separates you from the amateurs. This leads to one major question. **How do you know you've found a Mole?** Well, in reality, the Mole finds you. The recruiting process is under her supervision. Through your interactions, you will naturally become a recognizable face in the jungle. As you spend quality time with your Favorite, enjoying your lap dances, and tipping with purpose, the Mole will be secretly observing your every move. It may seem unlikely, but she's not motivated by acquiring your business. She has no desire to compete with your Favorite. Instead of dollar signs, there is only admiration in her eyes. She may have overheard your Favorite gushing about your witty sense of humor, or a waitress might have expressed her excitement about seeing you stroll through the door. Either way, she embraces your Regular status. She can tell that you have a clear agenda, and you stick to it, no matter what. Once you start to have friendly chitchats, a unique connection will occur.

Oddly enough, you will start to build a friendship purely based on respect. The conversation is real and eliminates the need to read between the lies. You both will discuss the strip club game and the challenges that patrons and predators face in the jungle. Truthfully, she's content with being the "cool" stripper. For this reason, you always drizzle her with tips and order her drinks when the situation presents itself.

At some point, she will slide you her contact information. That's when you know that your Mole is reporting for duty.

SURVIVOR NOTE

Inside information will allow you to save face, money, and potential headaches. But in the jungle where you have few allies, that type of intel is hard to come by. Acquiring a trusted Mole can help you stay ahead of a game that wants to keep you in the dark.

LAW
19

WHAT HAPPENS IN THE JUNGLE,
STAYS IN THE JUNGLE,
AND
WHAT HAPPENS IN VIP,
NEVER HAPPENED

Despite the mainstreaming of strip clubs
and the new-age acceptance of the stripper
profession, visiting a jungle for a rendezvous is still a
private affair. Your appearance doesn't deserve a
public announcement; you are not making a giant
leap for mankind. From coast to coast, many of you
have unfortunately acquired a nightclub mentality.
Your goal is to socialize, seek attention, and frolic
around like its prom night. You act as if a VIP

booth is the same as a photo booth, and you can't wait to post your pictures for the world to see. Needless to say, the jungle is far from a nightclub.

Do not get caught up in the mirage created by exotic clubs. Their job is to blur the line and keep the place packed with partygoers, regardless of the fact that they are a nightclub disguised as a jungle. All you have to do is take a glance on their social media accounts, and you can find evidence of the hoax. There's pictures of the entire room, patrons, and all. Everyone there standing around a campfire, awkwardly waiting for a mysterious summon to sing "Kumbaya." You can spot groups of civilians, women who are acting like they're having a good time, but they're secretly observing the behavior of every male patron, taking notes, and mentally passing judgment. There's also video proof of bottle sparklers, further exposing the venue's true identity. Look closely, and through the camouflage, you can detect glamorized go-go dancers playing their part; also called stage dancers that love to hide on stage and avoid contact.

The truth is that some club owners wouldn't mind turning this private sanctuary into a public forum. They feel that the only way to sustain a business is to reinvent the wheel. Creating an intimate environment that fosters the relationship between a Regular and a Favorite is considered old-fashioned. The belief in merging the nightclub and the strip club is a definite sign of the times. And some unprincipled patrons wouldn't mind being treated like a number, standing in line, and promoting the exotic club facade. But a pure jungle is an exotic escape from the civilian world; a defection from the nightclub crowd. It's a private place for relaxation and a break away from routine. Similar to the motto of Las Vegas, what happens in the jungle, stays in the jungle.

It is one thing to discuss the inner workings of the jungle from a survival standpoint, but it is far more disturbing to expose the personal interactions within the jungle.

The same way it is customary to protect the personal identity of strippers, equal importance should be placed on respecting the personal space and privacy of your fellow patrons. It doesn't matter if you're an average Joe or a bonafide celebrity, both patrons should be afforded the privacy to have a good time without a cell phone hidden in the shadows. This manly stance would seem like a no-brainer. The only thing flashing should be a set of fake boobs.

If a famous NBA athlete with a signature beard happens to enter the jungle, that's not the time to turn into a male groupie and grab your phone and start a group chat. Leave the hero worship for the strippers, waitresses, and bartenders. Let them go into a feeding frenzy, but you stay focused and stick to your needs. If he decides to make it rain, quickly find shelter with a hungry stripper and deal with her. That's not the time to marvel at his rainmaking skills and act like you're at a fan fest. If you come face-to-face with that popular figure, give that baller a quick head nod, and go back to surviving. That move garners respect. But these are troubling times, where a rookie will have no shame violating a celebrity's space and asking for a picture while he's enjoying a lap dance from a sexy Tiger with perfect curves.

It's incomprehensible, but this sacred layer has been invaded by the lowest animal in the jungle; the rat. Some may think it's the snake, but snakes don't squeal and carry cell phones. The rat is also known as the Strip Club Informant. This patron can be anyone, even a member of your entourage. If the first half of this law rubs you the wrong way, then there's a good chance that you are the culprit.

The informant lives lawlessly with no logical purpose and no sensible agenda other than to spread gossip and create strip club drama. Not only do they have no intentions of getting a lap dance, making it drizzle, or engaging with a predator, but they'd rather spend the majority of their time observing your behavior. While you're watching the amazing pole work, they're watching you. As you sit mesmerized, staring at the twerk show, they're watching you. Instead of creating lustful memories, they're collecting information and writing it down in their mental notebook. If you make the mistake of telling them an intimate story, they can't wait to run back and tell the participants and civilians what you said. For them, absolutely nothing stays in the jungle. They make it their business to know your business so that they can pass it along to whoever validates their pathetic existence.

In the age of social media, where the majority of people assume that everyone shares the same narcissistic desire to reveal any and everything about their lives, the Strip Club Informant violates basic strip club etiquette. This cardinal rule applies to the fraternity and (sorority) of patrons.

Do unto others as you would have them do unto you.

It's saddening to witness the lack of common courtesy in the average strip club goer. You have rookies and unruly spectators posting pictures and capturing private moments in the jungle while violating others' privacy without regard. Some are so preoccupied with secretly taking selfies that DJs have to grab the microphone and state the obvious. Strippers are confiscating cell phones and annoyingly deleting pictures. This behavior is repulsive and morally destructive regarding strip club etiquette.

Does one ever think about the patron who is married, or the one on a business trip who doesn't want to be plastered over the Internet? What about the patron who is stressed out and simply wants time alone? What about the stripper with the side-job who wants to keep her life in the jungle separate from the concrete jungle? Shouldn't she have the right to decide what gets exposed? What happened to respecting one's privacy?

The focus should be on predators and living in the moment, not capturing the moment. Inside the jungle, anonymity is customary. A trip to the jungle is not an episode of a gossipy, tell-all reality show. Save your photo opportunities and videos for the nightclub.

For the owners and managers who operate a true jungle, it's only smart to take advantage of social media. Gone are the days when one flashy neon sign can symbolize a monopoly on all strip club business. Competition is at an all-time high. There are so many jungles battling for dollars that the list of establishments is longer than the Amazon River. Whether posting a real-time roll call, booty shake videos, or just promoting dance specials, the market forces jungles to adapt and use all avenues at their disposal for advertising purposes.

Strippers are also feeling the intense competition. The importance of name recognition has created a boom in twerk videos and thirst traps. Pictures of strippers receiving the green carpet treatment and counting money at the end of the night have become the norm. One simple shout-out by a trendy rapper can boost one's popularity and bank account overnight. Every other day, a new photoshoot is posted with the intention of luring you into the jungle. It is very common to find a club's main page flooded with snapshots of dancer profiles; tattoos and curves on display. This type of marketing is a reflection of the times, and as long as strippers give their consent; it's all part of the game. But this does not give you or any patron an excuse to use social media for exploitative reasons—stay in your lane!

If you are the type of patron that can't mind your own business, please do others a favor and stay away from the jungle. Take your talebearing ways to the nightclub and babble with the gossipers. The jungle is to be treated as a sacred ground, and respect and privacy are at the foundation of its existence.

WHAT ABOUT THE VIP ROOM?

Whether watching a predator seductively walk upstairs or disappear down a long corridor, every patron loves to imagine what's happening in the darkness of a VIP room; the mystery, the intrigue, and the possibility of a raunchy time is the stuff of strip club legend. And when a patron finally returns from the green mile, you can't help but wonder what type of battle scars he earned. How did he manage to survive the encounter? Did he suffer from a bout of VIP Stockholm syndrome? If so, will that traumatic experience turn him into a walking ATM? Even though the aftermath of a 30-minute VIP can have devastating consequences; good or bad, your inner savage will never allow you to be content with being on the outside looking in. No one in his or her right mind enters the jungle to be a spectator or a wallflower. Curiously, you want to know what you're missing out on. But whatever extracurricular activity happens in VIP should stay between you and the stripper. No matter how mind-blowing, shameful, or improbable the experience, the encounter stays in VIP. In fact, those exploits never happened—get the hint. It's understandable to have the biggest grin in the world or the coldest blank stare during the affair, but make sure you leave with a normal, calm demeanor—you're a professional and it's just another day at the office.

The second half of this law should be a dose of common sense, especially given that part of your agenda should be to maintain your lustful relationship and enjoy a repeat performance. But for many who enter the jungle to avoid boredom, keeping a tight lip on a crazy encounter is a daunting challenge. It's a natural tendency to want to spread the good news and everyone loves to hear a juicy, exclusive strip club story. Just look at the faces of your entourage, they can't wait to hear the lowdown between you and the stripper with the tongue piercing. Those early morning VIP confessions that happen around a huddle in the parking lot are fodder for comedians and screenwriters. Even outsiders love to eavesdrop and tell exaggerated tales of debauchery.

However, a seasoned veteran sees the bigger picture and resists the temptation to leak information. As a loyal patron, you must think about the long-term consequences of exposing what happens behind the velvet curtain. It's vital to understand that VIP also stands for Very Important Protocol—especially when it comes to the need for discretion. Unless you are entering a jungle called Club Tattle-Tails, take a moment to digest the reason why establishments started using the name Gentlemen's Club. A gentleman doesn't kiss and tell. Only little boys find enjoyment in being a chatty patty. What happens in the jungle, should stay in the jungle, and what happens in VIP, never happened.

Spreading the intimate details of extracurricular activities can harm the reputation of your trusted stripper and spoil your privileged status. Before you know it, a friend of yours is asking her for the same treatment—and that's not a good look for you and your crew. You shouldn't have to remind yourself that you purchased the time in VIP; it wasn't a group purchase. You didn't create a fundraiser page and promise your investors a first listen on your lap dance experience. There's absolutely nothing respectable about being messy and creating strip club drama. Real strippers that respect the game have no time for those that can't conduct themselves within the rules of engagement.

What strippers, like all women, do respect is a closed mouth. They respect discretion and one's privacy. You should too!

By and large, being a whistleblower can also affect the overall business of the club that your private encounter took place; the same club that you frequent and support with your hard-earned money. Remember, steamy details can easily become forwarded tips given to state officials and agencies that would love to start a fire in the jungle. Who wants to be responsible for instigating an undercover investigation? How can you endorse the hierarchy of needs without a fully functioning club? A survivor knows to never bite the hand that feeds him and singing like a canary is a lose-lose situation for all parties. Be an adult and keep things in-house.

Always maintain a *business never personal* attitude when it comes to private affairs. Would you like a stripper to post your name and personal information on the Internet for everyone to see? No. Let alone, blabber about your fetishes and dirty secrets that she learned while you were tipsy in VIP? Hell no. You don't want her to air out your dirty laundry, so lead by example and show her that you can have a lapse of memory. That way, you ensure yourself more memories to come.

SURVIVOR NOTE

Let the outsiders and civilians gossip and speculate about what happens in the darkness of the jungle. Their imaginations will always assume the worst, anyway. Just plead the fifth, stick to your agenda, and keep surviving. Talk is cheap and spilling secrets gains you zero advantage in a world of discretion.

LAW
20

THE ONLY TRUE SPECIAL
EVENT IS HALLOWEEN

In American culture and around the globe, it's a tradition to throw parties around sporting events, special occasions, and perceived holidays. It's no surprise that jungles proudly carry on this tradition, albeit with an ulterior motive. The fact is, a "special event" is a clever way to mirage a jungle's truthful purpose. It's the perfect cover-up; it's the unsuspected booby trap. It's like the action comedy movie *Tropic Thunder*, you think it's all for shits and giggles, but you're actually in the middle of a war zone. Once you get hooked on the theme or distracted by the flyer, you forget that you're walking into a jungle full of predators and the real special event is your sacrifice. Do you think that Taco

Tuesday is about the tacos? Do you think that
Amateur Night is really about showcasing new
talent? Veterans know that the majority of girls are
leopards and ringers, so who's the real *amateur* for
the night?

It's easy to crack a smile and applaud the
marketing strategies shown by managers and staff.
Competition never sleeps and what's a jungle
without patrons? A shutdown jungle.

That's why the list of promoted events is
never-ending. There are your weekly traps; Sam's
Monday's, Taco Tuesday, Woman Crush
Wednesday, Bottle & Bricks Thursday, Freaky
Friday, Seductive Saturday, and Sinful Sunday.
Then, you have your monthly mirages; Valentine's
Day, St. Patrick's Day, Cinco De Mayo, Father's
Day, Independence Weekend (Red, White, and
Boobs), Thanksgiving Bash (Breast, Thighs, and
Legs), and Naughty or Nice Secret Santa.

There are several theme parties; 80's Night,
Wet T-Shirt Contest, Naughty Schoolgirl Night,
Amateur Night, and so on.

Jungles even lure you in using the zodiac.
You can talk astrology with a predator that's a real
scorpion! Whatever the occasion, the invite will
never indicate the true intentions of the event. But
at the end of the day, everyone loves an excuse to
socialize and gather around the campfire. Even
though, patrons lose sight of what's hidden in the
dark.

As far as special events, there are only a few that have advantages. They provide creative ways to have a little fun while you're still surviving.

Promotional Events. These events are perfect if you're supporting a brand or artist. It's like a private party that you can actually attend. Although, after a couple of drinks, you'll be looking to promote your own brand of business; mainly the laws and endorsing the hierarchy of needs.

Sporting Events. Mega-popular events like the Super Bowl, World Series, and the NBA Finals bring out the inner fanatic in patrons and strippers. The rap artist Future single-handedly turned March Madness into a strip club event with his song that carries the same title. These sporting events have everyone glued to the television watching every second and wearing jerseys representing their team and favorite players. The tailgate party vibe is evident, and if your team wins, there's no better way to celebrate than getting a lap dance from a stripper who can give you a post-game recap. If your team loses, you can also find a MILF that will console you and let you know that you're a winner in her eyes.

Industry Nights. These weekly events can be a great time if you're truly there to network and schmooze—that's the selling point, right? But everyone knows that once a certain song comes on, one would rather rub shoulders with Emmy and Miami.

Porn Star Features. Porn stars always bring a magical energy to the jungle. Witnessing your favorite porn star up close and personal is like spotting a unicorn. It's a surreal experience, especially when you start to envision the sexual exploits that you've seen on-screen. For some patrons, this is the ultimate jungle story. Once in a blue moon, a unicorn will make an appearance, perform a few shows on stage and then disappear into the mythical darkness. Just don't expect her to provide the greatest show on Earth. Her expertise is in providing extracurricular activity. If you want a lap dance, a signed autograph or a personal photo, make sure you bring enough cash. Unicorns like to be paid extra for their magical qualities.

Pay-Per-View Fights. These celebrated pugilistic events bring an overly aggressive crowd that would rather watch two guys brawl than focus on Suzy and Marilyn with the MMA (Most Massive Ass). But most understand the popularity of boxing and mixed martial arts, so focused patrons just relax and experience the sports bar feel without complaint. And strippers love to watch their favorite fighters go at it. It exposes their animal instincts. However, one of the drawbacks is paying an annoyingly higher cover for a fight that might last 12 seconds.

New Year's Eve. This annual event could be fun, especially if you ring in the new year with champagne and high mileage. But emotions run high, and you could start to reminisce about all the money you lost on Air Dances and the strippers that are long gone and retired from the game. You might sneak a peek at their social media accounts and get a little teary-eyed. But you know that there are more predators in the jungle. You raise a toast and look forward to becoming a more seasoned survivor. Two of your new year's resolutions are to find a new Favorite and avoid the grumpy and bitter, but just like any new goal—it's always easier said than done.

HALLOWEEN

Although those events are just another reason to venture into the jungle and test your skills, there is only one event that keeps you focused on the stage. It's also sinfully sexy. A day when some predators with fangs turn into, well, predators with fangs—that event is Halloween. It's one of most popular days of the year and adults make sure that kids aren't the only ones trick-or-treating.

In the civilian world, some women take this day as an opportunity to let their hair down and dress more provocatively. They let loose and expose a different side of their normal, everyday persona. Regardless of how silly or creative the costume, for some reason, sexual expression always finds a way to creep out to the forefront. The streets become flooded with skimpy outfits and sexy characters, enough to make men howl at the moon like werewolves. But respectful gentlemen know that you can look—but don't touch. Just because you're dressed up as a monster doesn't mean you need to play the part. However, inside the haunted jungle, you can trick and receive a treat. The jungle is the only place where getting body snatched is not a bad thing.

Halloween, by far, is the most interactive special event. The attention is on the strippers and their hair-raising costumes—exactly where it should be. They're the focal point, the promoted brand, the industry insiders, the groups of unicorns, and the real pay-per-view special. Instead of watching a flat screen, or living vicariously through someone sitting in the front row of the MGM (Grand Garden Arena), the main event is right there in front of you. Who needs the Super Bowl halftime show, when you can watch the sexiest costume contest? For all you hardcore sports fans, here's one guarantee— whatever sports athlete you're obsessing over will never give you a high mileage lap dance wearing a Pocahontas outfit.

Halloween is one of the most playful atmospheres a club can provide. Along with hearing

"Thriller" 100 times, it brings out a mischievous spirit, an uninhibited thirst for naughty fun. Even the waitresses join in and provide candy to patrons. But strippers are ready to offer much more than candy. On this spooky night, lap dances reach devilish levels, depending on her costume and alter ego. Sophisticated patrons know that behind every costume is a hint of truth. Some strippers make last minute decisions, but the majority plan their costumes well in advance. You can learn a lot about a stripper by her costume choice. Instead of reading between the lies, you are reading between the costumes. Halloween is a rare time when they can let their personality show along with their sexuality. The stripper with the Double D's might want to show her inner nerd and become a librarian. Or that quiet, girl-next-door type might want to tap into her secret sassy side and turn into Jessica Rabbit. Or the stripper who does makeup on the side might want to show off her skills as a female Freddy Krueger.

Halloween is also the ideal time for role-playing. Strippers love to show off their acting skills. When you're suffering from a case of blue balls, who doesn't want to receive urgent care from Nurse Ratched? This event is the only time when you wouldn't mind getting strip searched by a sexy cop and hoping for excessive force. Considering the number of costumes, the possibilities of her playing out a flirtatious fantasy is endless. Outside of necrophilia, you can let your imagination reach Wes Craven levels. Turn the tables, and enjoy a rare moment of being the predator. You're now Dracula with a black cape looking for a victim, or a deviant doctor examining ass shots and boob jobs. A patron can transform from a clueless spectator to an accomplished hunter with one cool costume and some candy corn. That's what makes Halloween special.

SURVIVOR NOTE

There is no eye candy like the eye candy given inside a jungle on Halloween. Those treats you can unwrap immediately. Halloween is the perfect time to have freaky fun without masking your agenda.

LAW
21

EARN YOUR STRIPES
IN LAS VEGAS

Several cities are well known for their
jungles: Miami, Tampa, Detroit, Portland, Los
Angeles, City of Industry (a suburb of Los Angeles
that deserves to be mentioned), Chicago, Atlanta
(Home of the Strip Club Veterans), New York,
Houston, and Dallas. But there is one city that
stands out from the rest and it's not because of the
bright lights on the strip. This territory is the jungle
of all jungles; Las Vegas. Though it was once a
gangster's paradise, Vegas has transformed into a
family friendly haven for shows, restaurants, and
events. But for those willing to venture out and
observe the wild animals, there is no better place to
learn the ropes. The city of sin could also be called

the City of Survival. Once you get past the desert, you become Captain Willard in the movie *Apocalypse Now* sent on a mission into Cambodia with a clear objective, but somehow, things take a drastic turn, and now your mission is making it out alive—that's Las Vegas. Gamblers aren't the only ones who catch the bug and get their pockets cleaned out. Many strip club patrons leave Vegas shell-shocked with physical and psychological damage.

There are so many jungles that you will need a comprehensive travel guide just to locate each establishment and prepare you adequately for your excursion. Vegas is the place where you earn your stripes; it's by far the most dangerous playground to test your survival skills. Jungles like Sapphire, the world's biggest strip club, the luxurious Crazy Horse III and the ruling Spearmint Rhino turn the most accomplished explorers into bumbling tourists upon entry. Treasures is another jungle that provides more than enough booty, and Club Paradise is the perfect trap for travelers looking for a heavenly experience, only to walk into the belly of the beast. Patrons learn within seconds that only the most aggressive predators inhabit and migrate to Vegas.

Even some of the top moneymakers from Miami, Houston, Atlanta, and other cities shy away from Vegas. They talk about working there, it's an item on their stripper bucket list, but it's funny how that destination remains a lofty goal. They conjure up excuses that clubs won't hire them based on their look and figure, or they say that there's too much cattiness among felines. They hear stories about the cannibalistic nature of predators that backstab and take advantage of the weak. The truth is that most are afraid to work side by side with hustlers that will make them step up their game. They're also hesitant to entertain strip club aficionados that are animalistic and hip to the ways of the jungle. They know that Vegas is the place where Sugar Daddies and Whales flex their muscles and give sinful offers that are tough to refuse. Temptation takes on a whole new meaning when you can hide your actions in the dark and bury the remains in the desert. It's all in the famous slogan—the city is based around secrecy. Most predators would rather stay at their home club and continue intimidating familiar faces that aren't as savage.

Although the most famous jungles in Vegas can afford to be picky with their rosters, several managers can't wait to hire those that can handle the heat and humidity. In this city, the stakes are higher, and competition is top notch. There's no other environment as rich in greenery and prosperity. Only a chosen few can even attempt to make it rain in Vegas. Unless you are one of the greatest boxers of all time and you have a girl collection, only then can you play by your own rules. But for the average patron, throwing dollars in the air is pointless in a room full of money. Furthermore, these predators want more than rain.

For these go-getters, being money-hungry is an understatement. They want assets, credit cards, shopping sprees, exotic trips, as well as your soul. Don't worry. If you can't apply for Sugar Daddy status, they'll gladly accept an application for temporary sponsorship. It's all part of the game.

For those who are unfamiliar with the treacherous terrain, here are a few reasons why Vegas is the most intense jungle of them all.

ECOSYSTEM DIVERSITY

First of all, no other city can compare to the influx of predators that travel from all over the globe in search of money and prey; two things that are always in season. You think New York's ecosystem is diverse with strippers from different countries? Vegas is the Miss Universe pageant with every country represented during the swimsuit competition. Every type of wild animal on the planet is on display. The sexiest Brazilians, Colombians, and the rest of South America all roam the jungles looking for prey. Dominicans and Puerto Ricans don't only dominate the New York scene; they're also in Vegas increasing the competition. New York has a strong presence of Russians, but Vegas has representatives from all ten countries of Eastern Europe. Do you want to get a lap dance by a model type from the Czech Republic, or Slovakia? Have you ever gotten a killer lap dance from a Tiger from Bulgaria? One who pushed aside her dreams of becoming a model and flew straight to Vegas for the money. The average patron rarely gets to encounter this type of predator.

There are Asians, Canadians, Australians, Africans, and any other region you can imagine. These aren't predators from your neighborhood. And by no means are we to overlook the strippers from the states. If you've never been to a club in the Midwest, you'll be sure to bump into a seductive predator from Wisconsin. Have you ever met a Tiger from Missouri? How about a stripper from South Dakota? Kentucky? Maine? You can get a taste from any club in the US, right there in Vegas.

This influx is every day and every night. Not to mention Super Bowls, boxing fights, MMA events, porn conventions, concerts, and whatever excuse there is for carnivores to swoop in like Vultures, snatch up prey and fly back to their hideouts.

FREE TRIPS TO THE JUNGLE

Vegas gives you a greater emphasis on Law 2, Always Plan Your Entrance And Exit. Just getting to your destination is a strategic decision that carries consequences. Exiting is another challenge.

If you decide to drive, make sure you contact the club ahead of time, there's a good chance they will waive your entry fee. They admire the effort of those who get behind the wheel—that's dedication. It's also a risk if you plan on getting hammered and driving home.

If you intend on taking a taxi, don't be surprised if the driver tries to persuade you to visit another establishment. It'll just so happen to be a location that pays the driver a significant commission for delivering vulnerable prey. Ensure that you stick to your plan and avoid detours to jungles you haven't researched.

One of the biggest signs that you're in the belly of the beast is that several jungles will send you a limo or shuttle bus for a pickup. This patron friendly option is just an example of how sinister jungles are in Vegas. They know exactly what they're doing. They'll throw in some perks like free admission and drink discounts to keep you distracted from the fact that you're being escorted into a pit of quicksand. It's no coincidence that most clubs will help get you there, but they won't help you escape.

HUSTLER'S PARADISE

Inside the jungle is where the hustle intensifies. Reading between the lies is extremely challenging when you're dealing with a predator that flew in for the weekend. Most predators in Vegas are nomadic; their home club is miles away. Unless you live in Vegas, you don't have the luxury to spend several days, weeks, months, years, evaluating a target. Usually, you could perfect the drizzle and let the interest mature. But every interaction in Vegas demands immediate attention. Time is money, and things go faster when there's no clock on the wall. The pressure is on, and you're rolling the dice, betting on your instincts. You must listen carefully, react quickly, and take advantage of the moment. Your level of inquisitiveness has to be on a Sherlock Holmes level. You're not only dealing with a stage name and a stripper persona; now you can encounter a person with a whole new identity. You'll never know if she's ever telling the truth.

Although this book does not condone being an actor, even though you are dealing with an actress, Vegas is the perfect place to play a fictional role in your own adventure. Being a local is considered boring and predictable, and most predators assume that locals are just spectators with alligator arms. Having a *story* keeps it fun and mysterious. Just make sure that your bank account can back up your claims of being a major league baseball player or a budding actor.

Exaggeration and overselling is part of the hustle. You will hear every sales pitch in the book. A place of high-stakes usually translates to high mistakes! And choosing wisely becomes a matter of life and death. You can find yourself $400 in the hole before you even receive a quality lap dance.

There are three lap dancers in particular that you have to watch out for. These predators wreak havoc in the jungles of Las Vegas.

The One-Night Stand Lap Dancer. This aggressive predator seductively sells you the fantasy of the greatest sexual escapade of a lifetime; a Vegas one-night stand. She's asking all the right questions. What hotel are you staying at? How long are you in town? What are you doing later? She even starts to tell you that she hasn't had sex in months. You start to think this is too good to be true. She doesn't shy away from touch either. With every move, she's giving you a hint of what could be. Her words are so tempting that you start to wonder if she will throw you a price. But it doesn't matter if you get caught up in the fantasy, she'll get her price regardless.

The City Slicker Lap Dancer. This predator happens to live in your city and she's visiting Vegas on a 2-day stint. Once you find out this bit of information, the conversation heats up as you discuss specific locations and details. You might even share the same devotion to your local sports team, or daringly talk about high schools and favorite hangouts. You two share an instant connection that breaks the ice. You can't help but fantasize about meeting up back home for some fun. And she knows this all too well. She's a slickster taking advantage of your thirst. Now she's offering her contact information, and hyping up a future date that she knows will never happen. Of course, this is while you're spending all your money in VIP.

The Party Pooper Lap Dancer. This predator is a slight variation of the Rule Enforcer mentioned in Law 8, Choose Wisely: It's More Lap And Less Dance. But instead of lecturing you on the rules of the club, she wants to tell you how she's not like all the other predators in Vegas. Not only is she running down a list of things that she won't do, the party pooper assumes that every patron wants to pay for sex. But you haven't even mentioned anything about extracurricular activity. The lap dance has barely started and she's already ruined the vibe. Her primary goal is not to deliver a sinful experience, but to make you feel guilty for wanting to have a good time in Vegas, of all places.

24 HOURS OF ENDLESS DANGER

Mastering the art of timing takes on a whole new meaning in Vegas. Some of the most dangerous jungles are open 24 hours. At any time of the day, you can get ambushed by the most exotic predators. You can skip breakfast and have a fantastic time looking at hotcakes at eight o'clock in the morning, or you skip dessert, arrive at midnight, and still have to wait for the apex predators to show up. In any other city, you can take advantage of the differences between the Day-Shift and Night-Shift. But in Vegas, time and space are warped. It's extremely difficult to determine the peak-hours—prime time is what you make it. The bright lights do bring out more nocturnal strippers, but in reality, most predators are cathemeral. They take quick power naps and then wake up and go back hunting. So in essence, there's just one long shift. Once you highlight the fact that there's no 'last call for alcohol,' it's no wonder why the lines between day and night are blurred. As a result, the lap dances never stop, and the drinks keep flowing like the Congo River. It's not uncommon for some patrons to go into a jungle and come out two days later.

POST TRAUMATIC SPRUNG DISORDER (PTSD)

If you're a fresh 18-year-old going to Vegas, that's the equivalent of being drafted into the Vietnam War. You'll be dropped off in the middle of Little Darlings without a clue of what's in store. Even though fully nude jungles do not serve alcohol, veterans quickly forget the intoxicating power of the naked body. Throw in 50-70 strippers with landing strips, piercings, and tattoos, and the experience is mind altering. Especially with the plastic surgery craze, some of these strippers' bodies are works of art. They've been sculpted to perfection or at least some have. Despite the dim light, once a rookie gets a glance at the goodies, his world will be turned upside down. The sexual atmosphere will stain his brain, bordering on perversion and overindulgence. From that point on, he will most likely suffer from chronic or acute *Post Traumatic Sprung Disorder* (*PTSD*). That's when you have a strip club experience so mind-blowing that one becomes traumatically sprung to the highest degree. It can happen anywhere, but Vegas is the #1 cause of this disorder. Regardless of age and level of strip club experience, anyone can be afflicted.

PTSD IS CHARACTERIZED BY THREE MAIN TYPES OF SYMPTOMS:

◆ Strong refusal to leave Vegas. Feelings of anxiety, excessive smiling, salivation, and inability to stop talking about the predators in the jungle. The time in Vegas was *a movie*. The mere thought of leaving triggers depression.

◆ Strong refusal to go back to Vegas. Persistent flashbacks cause fear and shame. Intense feelings of heartbreak and loss. Just the very mention of Vegas brings numbness, powerlessness, and despair. Irritable anger and depression towards the jungle and its predators.

◆ Tendency to compare the sex appeal of predators in Vegas (or any other jungle) to civilians in the real world. Inability to escape the fantasy of the jungle and not willing to live in reality. Unable to distinguish between the hustle of a predator and the regular dating process with a civilian. Strong desire to live or visit Vegas on a regular basis.

LAS VEGAS ITSELF IS A JUNGLE

What also separates Las Vegas from other well-known cities with jungles is that Vegas itself is a jungle. Your pockets are preyed upon everywhere you go. That's why many call it, "Lost Wages." You never really escape until you leave the desert. Even with that, Vultures still follow you, hoping that you collapse from dehydration. You may have thought you survived a jungle, only to walk into a casino and see more predators lurking around. You stroll into a high-end restaurant, and eyes are staring at you from every table. Stumble into a nightclub and felines are looking you up and down; some wild and some domesticated. Take a dip into a pool at a day club, and to your surprise, Piranhas are circling you. Keep in mind that all predators are not strippers. You have civilians on the hunt for free drinks, complimentary dinners, nightclub hookups, and an overall fun time at your expense. There are also the stationary predators: slot machines and card dealers. Their body count is endless. Last but not least, you have your occasional woman of the night, hoping that you fall victim to loneliness and temptation.

These facts make Vegas the largest and most intense jungle of them all.

SURVIVOR NOTE

If you can survive the jungles in Las Vegas, you can survive any jungle in the land. The stripes you earn in Sin City prepare you for the capitalistic and exploitative nature of the strip club industry. The stripes become battle scars that remind you that you can endure any challenge that comes your way and still stick to your agenda.

GLOSSARY

THE LANGUAGE OF THE JUNGLE

Some of these terms are well known throughout the inner circle of survivors; while others will be new additions to your strip club lexicon. Knowing the language of the jungle is equivalent to knowing the sounds of the jungle—it keeps you alert, aware, and on your toes. Being able to talk the talk, and walk the walk is a clear sign of a survivor.

AIR DANCE: A non-contact lap dance where there is so much air between you and the stripper that you feel deflated and utterly exploited. Unlike a table dance or a stage dance where no contact is customary, an Air Dance is usually unexpected and unsettling. It is the absolute worst dance a patron can receive.

AIR DANCE RIPPLE EFFECT: A situation where after a patron receives an unexpected Air Dance, the event causes the patron to buy a lap dance immediately from another stripper in hopes of replacing the void left by air. If the patron does not choose the right stripper, things can spiral out of control.

ATF: All-Time Favorite (See Favorite). The ATF is a term only reserved for a stripper who has reached the level of a jungle goddess.

BAIT AND SWITCH: The ploy of using a stack of cash (brick) as bait to attract strippers to a table, giving them the

185

illusion of a big payday, then switching up and only spending a small amount of cash.

BALLOON DANCE: A mini-lap dance given by a waitress where she places a balloon on your lap and grinds intensely until it pops. The balloon dance is typically done for a small charge or the cost of a beverage.

BIRD DOG: A bouncer whose unpopular job is to monitor the activity in the VIP area. This bouncer is on the hunt for savage patrons.

BLIND LAP: When a patron blindly rolls the dice and chooses a lap dance from a stripper whom they've never seen twerk, booty-shake, perform on stage, or give a lap dance.

BRICK: A stack of cash.

BUNNY RABBIT: A stripper that is a Professional Air Dancer. She is the prude of the jungle, prancing around and trying to avoid touches at all costs.

CATHEMERAL STRIPPER: A stripper that works during the Day and Night-Shift. Las Vegas has a thriving population of cathemeral strippers.

CF: Current Favorite (See Favorite).

CIVILIAN: The average woman who does not work in the jungle and likes to visit for so-called fun. Her only agenda is to secretly observe the behavior of male patrons.

CONCRETE JUNGLE: A general term used to describe the world outside the jungle. This world is also exploitative, capitalistic, and predatory.

DIURNAL STRIPPER: A stripper that primarily works during the Day-Shift.

THE ETERNAL PATRON DILEMMA: The tricky dilemma that a patron faces when trying to choose the right stripper for a lap dance that's worth the price. This challenge is the most crucial and monetarily volatile decision in the jungle.

EXTRACURRICULAR ACTIVITY: Use your imagination.

FAVORITE: 1. A patron's favorite stripper. Although a patron may claim to have several, only one will receive the majority of the patron's resources (time and money). 2. A Favorite is one of the two halves of the lustful union that makes up the core foundation of the strip club industry. The powerful yin and yang relationship between a Favorite and a Regular provides the energy flow that supports the entire strip club ecosystem.

GFE: Girlfriend Experience. Not to be confused with the full-fledged definition used in the world of high-end escorts and call-girls. In the jungle, this term describes an intimate connection between a patron and a stripper that goes beyond the typical business interaction. A Favorite usually offers a Girlfriend Experience to a Regular; long talks, neck massages, therapy sessions, warm hugs, an open ear, and a genuine concern for their well-being without the daily struggles of a girlfriend & boyfriend relationship.

GREEN CARPET TREATMENT: After a patron makes it rain, the floor or main stage becomes covered in cash, creating the appearance of a newly placed green carpet.

GREEN MILE: The long walk that a patron makes with a stripper to a VIP room.

HOME CLUB: A stripper's favorite jungle to hunt; a primary residence for a stripper who prefers not to leap from jungle to jungle like a leopard.

THE HONEST MISTAKE: When a shady waitress adds mysterious items to a patron's bill, hoping that the items go unnoticed and uncontested. This scam is done under the disguise of being an honest mistake. Ironically, the waitress is counting on the patron's honesty, assumed trust, and reluctance to dispute a bill publicly in front of strippers.

HOUSE MOM: An employee of the jungle that acts as a motherly figure and a personal assistant for strippers.

JANE: A stripper; as in Jane of the Jungle.

JILL: A waitress; the little sister of Jane of the Jungle.

JUNGLE: The appropriate name for a strip club. It represents the exploitative, capitalistic, and predatory nature of the strip club environment.

THE JUNGLE OF ALL JUNGLES: Las Vegas.

LAP DANCE: An erotic, intimate, one-on-one dance in which a stripper sits, caresses, grazes, or grinds a patron's lap for the duration of one song. Additional touching from both parties may take place based on the stripper, the shift, and the jungle. Tipping is optional.

LEOPARD: A nomadic stripper that's hard to capture because she is not tied down to a home club. She is always on the run, leaping from jungle to jungle, chasing the money.

MAKING IT DRIZZLE: An economical approach to tipping where a patron selects a primary stripper and tips her in steady increments, building up stripper equity. Just like a watering can, the patron lets the light rain trickle down, dollar by dollar. This approach is a clear alternative to making it rain.

MAKING IT RAIN: An extravagant, often gratuitous form of tipping where a patron tosses or peels off dollar bills in the air, creating the spectacle of rainfall.

MASSAGE GIRL: An employee of the jungle that gives patrons massages on the main floor for a charge. Tipping is customary and there is no happy ending.

THE MEDUSA EFFECT: A situation where a patron stares at a waitress (or bartender) for too long, in effect, turning to stone and falling victim to her allure. The patron becomes infatuated and begins only to visit the jungle for the sole purpose of trying to date the waitress.

MERCY TIP: A tip given to a stripper on stage purely out of sympathy because no other patron is tipping.

MILEAGE: A term that represents the amount of physical contact and extracurricular activity that a patron can get away with during a lap dance.

MILF: An acronym for Mother I'd Like to Fuck. Inside the jungle, a MILF is an older woman in her dirty 30's and filthy 40's with a kid or a few, who is a seasoned veteran with many years of stripping experience.

THE MOLE: A stripper (agent) that can give a patron inside information that will enable that patron to stay ahead of the game and maneuver around a strip club industry that is inherently cutthroat and constantly evolving.

NEWBIE: A young stripper who is learning the ropes and the ways of the jungle.

NOCTURNAL STRIPPER: A stripper that primarily works during the Night-Shift.

OUTSIDER: A person who is a staunch critic of strippers, and the strip club industry.

THE PATRON'S HIERARCHY OF NEEDS: The motivational theory that everything flows and revolves around the three-level pyramid of services. The coveted lap dance is at the top of the hierarchy of needs; followed by the table dance, and lastly, the stage dance. The three levels enable the patron to utilize their five senses (sight, hearing, smell, touch, and taste) to their maximum.

PIRANHA: An overly aggressive stripper that is relentless and ferocious in her approach. This type of stripper rolls in a pack and loves to attack VIP tables.

POLE WORK: A stripper's artistic, high-flying, gymnastic performance on a shiny stripper pole. Some strippers deserve gold medals for their Olympic pole work skills.

POST TRAUMATIC SPRUNG DISORDER

(PTSD): A mental condition triggered by experiencing a strip club event so mind-blowing that you become sprung to the highest degree. The symptoms are chronic or acute.

PREDATOR: A playful term for a stripper representing her predatory nature to prey on a patron's money, body, and soul.

RAINCOATER: An extreme pervert. The term was originally created to describe a dirty old man who entered an adult theater wearing a trench coat and barely anything underneath for the purpose of secretly playing with himself.

REGULAR: 1. A regular is a patron who frequents a jungle; a recognizable face that is familiar with the environment and its inhabitants. 2. Formerly considered a negative label (some consider being a Regular a pathetic loser), a Regular is one of the two halves of the lustful union that makes up the core foundation of the strip club industry. The powerful yin and yang relationship between a Favorite and a Regular provides the energy flow that supports the entire strip club ecosystem.

RINGER: An experienced stripper who purposely visits a foreign jungle for Amateur Night, especially if there is a cash prize.

ROOKIE: A young, misguided, and agenda-less patron who is naive to the ways of the jungle.

SABBATICAL: A hiatus, typically a few months, taken when a stripper gets plastic surgery.

SIMPLETON: A foolish patron that lacks the common sense and awareness to understand that one's survival is at stake. This patron thinks everything is fun and games, and being economical is silly.

SPECTATOR: A patron who simply watches all the activity in the jungle with no plans of getting their hands dirty or spending money.

STAGE DANCE: A no-contact stage performance by a stripper where patrons can only admire and salivate over a neoclassic striptease. Tipping is customary.

STAGE DANCER: A title that represents a stripper that prefers only to perform on stage. The use of this title is an indirect way of indicating to a patron that she is not a fan of giving lap dances.

STAGE FEE: A fee that strippers pay to work in the jungle. Unlike employees, strippers are independent contractors who have to pay to take advantage of an atmosphere that provides the paying patrons.

STARTENDER: A pseudo-bartender who thinks she's the main attraction; the star of the jungle.

STRIP CLUB ACCOUNTANT: The patron in charge of calculating and categorizing every expense. This is the last job you want in the jungle, especially in a big party. No one wants to talk about the budget.

STRIP CLUB ECOSYSTEM: The entire community of living inhabitants of the jungle; strippers, waitresses, the DJ, bartenders, restroom attendants, valet, managers, bouncers, etc.

STRIP CLUB FOOD CHAIN: The natural pecking order of all living inhabitants of the jungle, but mainly between the stripper, waitress, and bartender. Patrons (producers), who provide the cash (energy) do no visit the jungle to see or interact with any other inhabitants. The stripper is at the top of the food chain as the apex predator, the waitress is a secondary predator, and the bartender is a primary predator.

STRIP CLUB INFORMANT: A patron whose agenda is to collect information for the purpose of spreading gossip and creating strip club drama.

STRIPPER ECOSYSTEM: The micro-community of strippers that inhabit the jungle; every type of species imaginable competing for patrons, survival, and prosperity.

STRIPPER EQUITY: The amount of interest (time and money) invested into a stripper with the expectation of return.

STRIPPER FOOD CHAIN: The natural pecking order of strippers who eat within the jungle based on power, popularity, and hustle. Apex predators are at the top of the food chain and Vultures are the scavengers at the bottom of the food chain.

STRIPPER GAMESMANSHIP: The mental and physical chess game that strippers play on patrons by using seductive ploys and tactics to gain any advantage they can when it comes to extracting a patron's money. Some Regulars call this "Stripper Game" or "Stripper Shit" concerning to the lies and stories that strippers tell to get patrons to fork over their cash.

SUGAR DADDY: An older man (usually well-off) who financially sponsors a young woman's extravagant lifestyle in exchange for companionship.

SURVIVOR: A patron who thoroughly understands the 21 laws and adapts to any challenge in the jungle, regardless of the type of club and location. This patron knows the benefits of tipping, the importance of customer service, and respects the stripper's hustle.

TABLE DANCE: An Air Dance performed on a patron's table where one is close enough to touch, but only relegated to looking up in awe. Tipping is customary.

TARGET: A stripper who's on a patron's radar. The patron is locked in and ready to engage.

TIGER: An attractive stripper that is almost too good to be true. She combines beauty and hustle like no other, and the fact that this powerful feline won't be around for long makes her the biggest catch in the jungle.

TIGER STRIPES: A colorful and more appreciative term for stretch marks.

TIP OUT: A tip that most jungles require strippers to give employees, typically the DJ, bouncers, managers, and bartenders. Every jungle has different requirements.

TIP RAIL: The seating area around the stage where you can tip and admire the stage show. Historically, a tip was placed on a golden brass rail that served as a barrier between the patron and stripper. Tipping is mandatory.

TRICKLE-DOWN ECONOMICS: The theory based on the premise that within the jungle, making it drizzle, not making it rain is the most efficient way to create stimuli and build stripper equity. By concentrating your resources on a single stripper, tipping her directly in increments (trickles) minimizes risk while providing the best return on your investment.

UNICORN: A porn star. Once in a blue moon, a porn star will make a magical appearance in the jungle.

V.I.P.: An alternative acronym that means Very Important Protocol. This acronym is a reminder of the importance of privacy and discretion when it comes to the activity in the VIP room.

VIP STOCKHOLM SYNDROME: A psychological phenomenon when a patron is lured into a VIP room and stuck in there for hours, getting fleeced for all their money, and somehow, the patron expresses extreme sympathy for the stripper and her economic plight. Despite the enormous amount of money spent, the patron feels the stripper got the raw deal.

VULTURE: A general term for a stripper that mainly preys on the naiveté of rookies and simpletons. This type of stripper rarely attacks the lawful patron. The Vulture hovers around the front door and scavenges the main floor for those with mental weakness and uncontrollable lust.

WALK OF SHAME: The rarely discussed, shameful, and embarrassing walk out of a jungle after being cleaned out mentally, physically, and financially. Witnessing this depressing walk can affect a patron psychologically for months.

WHALE: A patron who has the deep pockets to swallow up a stripper and hold her hostage for several hours, especially in a VIP room. This beast of a patron is a nightmare for those who hesitate to stake their claim in the jungle.

INDEX

M

N

O

S